JORO'S YOUTH

THE FIRST PART OF THE MONGOLIAN EPIC OF GESER KHAN

TRANSLATED FROM THE MONGOLIAN VERSION OF 1716

JORO'S YOUTH

THE FIRST PART OF THE MONGOLIAN EPIC OF GESER KHAN

TRANSLATED FROM THE MONGOLIAN VERSION OF 1716

IGOR DE RACHEWILTZ AND LI NARANGOA

PRESS

Published by ANU Press
The Australian National University
Acton ACT 2601, Australia
Email: anupress@anu.edu.au
This title is also available online at press.anu.edu.au

National Library of Australia Cataloguing-in-Publication entry

Creator: De Rachewiltz, Igor, author.

Title: Joro's youth : the first part of the Mongolian epic of Geser Khan / Igor de Rachewiltz ; Li Narangoa.

ISBN: 9781760460822 (paperback) 9781760460839 (ebook)

Subjects: Gesar (Legendary character)
Epic literature, Tibetan--Translations into English.

Other Creators/Contributors:
Narangoa, Li, author.

Dewey Number: 895.41

Cover design and layout by ANU Press.

Director's Foreword

Professor Igor de Rachewiltz was a friend, colleague, and mentor of generations of scholars and students in the history of East Asia at The Australian National University for more than 60 years. For the last few years of his life, it was an honour and privilege that he chose to be based at the Australian Centre on China in the World. Ever supportive and stimulating, Igor's presence was a joy and an inspiration. It is a great sadness that he is lost to us all, but an immense satisfaction that we have been able to shepherd this last work of Igor's through ANU Press.

Benjamin Penny
Director
Australian Centre on China in the World
The Australian National University

Foreword

I had the privilege to work with Igor on this project. At the same time, I also feel very sad that this became our last project and that this will appear after his death. On 1 June 2016, Igor and I met Sharon Strange at the Australian Centre on China in the World (CIW) to sign the contract for publishing *Joro's Youth* — this very piece of translation. After signing the contract, we said 'ciao ciao' to each other because both of us had other appointments. I never thought that it would become our last meeting. It was Igor's wish to publish this book through CIW as a sign of his gratitude towards CIW for welcoming him as a member of its academic community.

I had the good fortune to get to know Igor over the last 15 years. We met regularly, almost every day when we had our offices next to each other for two to three years in the Coombs Building. He has been an inspiration to me personally as well as academically. Igor was a courtly gentleman who did remarkable things and brought charm and humour to everything he did. He was one of those classic scholars who had a breadth of knowledge well beyond his immediate fields and always had something intelligent to say on many subjects. He had such a positive and sunny energy that everyone around him enjoyed his company and learned something from him.

Igor was a great humanist. He started his academic career as a historian under the supervision of Professor C.P. Fitzgerald, a great sinologist, and wrote his thesis on Yelu Chusai (who was the advisor to Chingghis Khan, the ruler of the Mongol empire, and his successor) at the Department of Far Eastern History — the predecessor of the Department of Pacific and Asian History at The Australian National University. His main research work focused on 13th- and 14th-century history. His subsequent contribution to the field of Mongolian studies was monumental. The most extraordinary contribution he made was to publish an annotated translation of *The Secret History of the Mongols*.

It was a very difficult project that few could achieve: one has to be very good at medieval Mongolian and classical Chinese, as well as modern Mongolian, Russian, French, German, and Japanese, in which most scholarship on the Mongol empire has been written. Igor fulfilled all these conditions and did a superb job. It has not only been accepted as the standard translation of *The Secret History of the Mongols*, but the annotation alone is considered to be a scholarly treasure. It was not an ordinary work of translation; it consists of three volumes of nearly 2,000 pages. The translation itself consists of 220 pages, while the commentary on the translation is much more expansive — spanning 823 pages — and the rest is dedicated to an analytical introduction and historiography. For this monumental work, he was awarded the Denis Sinor Medal from the Royal Asiatic Society, and the Polar Star Medal of Mongolia, which is the highest honour given to a scholar by the Mongolian Government. Both of these were awarded in 2007. These are just a couple of the numerous academic awards and distinctions that he received from many countries and organisations as a world-recognised Mongolist.

Apart from his fascination for Chinggis Khan, he also had a great interest in Geser Khan, the ruler of the world in a Mongolian epic that has been considered an important part of Mongolia's cultural heritage. While he was still working on his second volume of *The Secret History,* we were talking about translating a short form of the Geser epic, for general reading. 'Short form' meaning just the main story lines without the descriptions repeated, which are common for Mongolian epic poems, but both of us were distracted by other projects and Igor soon started working on the third volume of *The Secret History*.

While Igor was working on the third volume, he said that he would be 'closing up shop', so to speak, after he completed the project and would then catch up on his Japanese. He was then 84 years old! Within a few days after submitting the third volume, he had a stroke. When he recovered, he told me in his very cheerful way that his doctor explained that he should continue working on his projects. He said that his 'next second-to-last' project would be taking up the Geser project that we had been talking about but as a more direct translation of the Mongolian Geser Khan epic text of 1716 'just for fun' — in other words, that there would not be any footnotes, or at least not extensive footnotes! He asked me if I would still be interested in joining him on the project and I instantly accepted his invitation. We met regularly to discuss the work and I was amazed at how well he understood the 18th-century Mongolian text, which is quite different from the 13th-century Mongolian that he used to work on. He was never afraid of spending time on his research no matter how trivial the matter was. Once he said 'producing good scholarship is like making yoghurt: the process cannot be hurried'.

I am extremely thankful to Igor for asking me to join him on this project. We worked on this translation for nearly two years and submitted the manuscript in early 2016. This project greatly benefited from the help and kind assistance of the following individuals: I would like to thank Hoang Oahn Collins, Igor's long-time research assistant, for word processing the translation; Ines de Rachewiltz, Igor's wife, for reading our draft translation and providing editorial help; Jonathan Ratcliffe for compiling the character list; Sharon Strange for assisting in liaising with the publisher and for proofreading; and Linda Allen for the copyediting.

Igor was also the most organised person I have ever known. He worked methodically on one project after another. He intended that his 'next second-to-last' project would be the Mongolian translation of the *Classic of Filial Piety* (*Xiao jing*), which is the only original Mongolian text that survived the Ming purge of Mongolian books. Unfortunately, he was not able to launch this project before he fell ill and went to see Chinggis Khan. It seems that his Chinggis Khan did not like him working on a Confucian text!

The field of Mongolian studies has lost a giant scholar and I have lost a dear friend, a respected mentor, and a valued colleague. Igor will live on among us through his fantastic work and the wonderful memories that he has left with us as his gift.

Li Narangoa
5 September 2016

List of Characters

Absa Kürje	Geser's heavenly grandmother.
Aju Mergen, daughter of the King of the Dragons	Geser's third wife. An Amazonian warrior figure.
Amin Sakigchi	Oldest son of Khormusda.
Arulga Goa, daughter of Ma Bayan	One of Geser's three wives. Her sister is **Machina Kimusun Goa** and her brother the revered **Chorisdong Lama**.
Asmai Noyan	A competitor against Geser in a horse race to win Rogmo Goa.
Bam Soyurja, son of Badmari	A great magician whose form Geser takes.
Boa Dongjong Garbo, Ariya Avalori Odkari and **Irjamsad (= Jamso) Dari Odam**	Three divine beings born from Amurchila along with Joro/Geser. They are destined to be the rulers of the highest gods, dragon kings, and *dakini* deities respectively.
Buddha Shakyamuni	Founder of Buddhism and highest divine being. His main purpose in the story is to have Khormusda promise to send someone to Earth to alleviate its sufferings.
Chargin, ruler of Dungsar	The most powerful of the three earthly rulers and a patron to Geser when he is in his form of Joro.

Chotong Noyan, ruler of Lig	The middle of the earthly rulers and main antagonist of the epic. Most of the action and humour in the story concerns Geser and his uncle trying to trick and outwit one another in a series of challenges.
Erlig Khan	The god of the underworld.
***Garuda*-bird**	A divine bird from Indic mythology. Retrieving its feathers in order to win a wife is a regular motif in Mongolian heroic epics.
Gegshe Amurchila, daughter of Kü Bayan	Joro/Geser's earthly mother who is taken prisoner by the three earthly lords, but because she is wounded is given to the lowly Sanglun to be his wife. She conceives Geser miraculously.
Güngü Echige Ergeslong (= Gelong) lama	A great lama who takes the form of a devil to try to kill Joro/Geser in his infancy. This devil-lama motif is common in both Tibetan and Mongolic versions of the Geser epic.
Jasa Shikir and **Rongsa**	Geser's older earthly half-brothers, the sons of Sanglun and an earlier wife.
Khormusda	King of the gods and heavenly father of the hero Geser. Originally Ahura Mazda, the God of Goodness in Zoroastrianism and introduced into Mongolian culture via Manichaeism. Associated with Brahma or Indra in Mongolian Buddhism.
King of the Dragons	A ruler of the lower world. Dragons here indicate the serpentine Naga of Indic mythology.
King of the Mountains Ua Günjid	A mountain deity.
Moa Güshi and **Dangbo**	Two wise soothsayers who foretell the incarnation of Geser and his sisters.

Rogmo Goa, daughter of Iskilü (= Senggeslü) Khan	Geser's main wife.
Sanglun, ruler of Tusa	The earthly father of Joro/Geser and lowest of the three earthly rulers.
Tegüs Chogtu	Youngest of the three sons of Khormusda.
Üile Bütügegchi	The middle son of Khormusda who comes to Earth to alleviate evil and suffering as the hero **Geser Khan.** Sometimes referred to by the full titles **Serbo Dongrub Lord of the Ten Quarters** or **The Merciful and Wise Geser Khan Uprooter of Evil in the Ten Quarters.** The name for the youthful form of Geser before he reveals his powers is **Snotty Joro**. The unsightliness of the young Geser is juxtaposed with the miraculous nature of his deeds, forming much of the appeal and humour in the story.
White Goddess Ariya Alamkari	A divine being who acts as the protectress of Geser on Earth.

Introduction

Some General Remarks

The year 2016 marked the 300th anniversary of two landmarks in the history of Mongolian literature and Chinese philology. It was in January/February and May respectively of the year 1716 that the Mongolian version of the Tibetan epic of Geser (in Tibetan Gesar) Khan and the famous Kangxi Dictionary (*Kangxi zidian*) were published in Peking.[1]

Although these two works bear no direct relationship to each other, they reflect the syncretic cultural outlook of the Manchu court and of the newly established Qing dynasty (1644–1911). The Kangxi emperor (r. 1662–1722), who sponsored both projects, was the first ruler of China to introduce a multilingual culture in the empire, with three languages, *viz.* Manchu, Chinese, and Mongolian being used for official purposes. Before the Qing, the Mongol rulers of the Yuan dynasty (1260–1367) had employed 'sundry aliens' (*semuren*) — mainly central and western Asian Muslims — in their administration of China, but the mediums used in official documents were usually a hybrid vernacular Chinese[2]

1 The date of the Mongolian version of 1716, the full title of which is *Arban jüg-ün ejen Geser qaγan-u tuγuji orosiba* (*Story of King Geser, Lord of the Ten Quarters* (hereafter GK)), that is, the 10 regions of the world (see Section II, n. 15), is found in the colophon of the blockprint, ch. 7, 5a; that of the *Kangxi Dictionary* at the end of the Kangxi emperor's preface to the dictionary. The importance of the former is that it is the first printed edition not only of the Mongolian version but of the Geser epos, and of the latter not the huge number of characters it contains (three quarters of which are of little or no use) but their classification under 214 'radicals' — a system of classification still valid today. See W. Heissig, *Die Pekinger lamaistischen Blockdrucke in mongolischer Sprache. Materialen zur mongolischen Literaturgeschichte, Göttinger Asiat. Forschungen* 2, Wiesbaden: Harrassowitz, 1954, 35–36 (35). Cf., however, below, n. 40.

2 That is, Early Mandarin influenced by Mongolian, many samples of which were published by Ed. Chavannes in *T'oung Pao* 5:1904, 357–447, 6:1905, 1–42; and 9:1908, 297–428. This language is described in M.A.K. Halliday, *The Language of the Chinese Secret History of the Mongols*, Oxford: B. Blackwell, 1959.

and Mongolian in 'Phags-pa script.[3] With a few notable exceptions, the Mongol ruling elite was not interested in the language and culture of its subjects, relying mainly on interpreters and translators.[4]

The Manchus, on the other hand, had, from the start, a cultural affinity with the Mongols because their script was the Mongolian vertical script they had adopted with slight modifications early in the 17th century.[5] Besides, Manchu and Mongolian, being both Altaic languages, have many grammatical features and lexical elements in common.[6] Political ties between the two peoples became especially relevant at the time of the Manchu conquest of China and the fall of the Ming dynasty in the first half of the 17th century. Concurrent with the acquisition and refinement of the Mongol script under the two Manchu pre-dynastic rulers Nurhaci and Ambahai (r. 1616–26 and 1627–43) was their commission of translating from Chinese into Manchu and from Manchu into Mongolian the Basic (= Imperial) Annals (*benji*) of the three alien dynasties of China, *viz.* the Khitan Liao (907–1115), the Jurchen Chin (1115–1234) and the Mongol Yuan (1260–1367) of the *Standard Histories* (*zhengshi*). This major project was completed in 1631 and presented to the throne in 1644, the first year of the reign of the Shunzhi emperor (1644–61), first Manchu emperor of China.[7] Two years before, under Nurhaci's son Abahai, the Tibetan version of the *Sutra of the Wise Man and the Fool* (*Do dzang-lun*), a famous collection of Buddhist stories, had been printed in its Mongolian version in Peking under the

3 On this script, devised by Khubilai Khan's (r. 1260–94) Tibetan adviser 'Phags-pa Lama (1235–80) in 1269, see G. Kara in P.T. Daniels and W. Bright, *The World's Writing Systems*, OUP, 1996, 437–41. Known also as the 'square script', 'Phags-pa's script, based on the Tibetan alphabet, is the world's first truly international alphabet.

4 See H. Franke, 'Could the Mongol Emperors Read and Write Chinese?', *Asia Major* 3:1953, 28–41; H. Franke and D. Twitchett, eds, *The Cambridge History of China. Vol. 6: Alien Regimes and Border States, 907–1368*, CUP, 1994, 560, 610, 624–27, and Hsiao Ch'i-ch'ing, *New Essays on the History of the Yuan Dynasty* (in Chinese), Taipei, 1999, 323–84.

5 See Daniels and Bright, *op. cit.*, 550–54. Cf. A.W. Hummel, ed., *Eminent Chinese of the Ch'ing Period (1644–1912)*, Washington: US Government Printing Office, 1943, 213, s.v. Dahai.

6 Manchu belongs to the Tungusic family of the Altaic languages and its correlation to Mongolian, a member of the Mongolic family, is still unclear. However, cf. G.D. Sanzheev, 'Man'čžuro-mongol'skije jazykovie paralleli' ('Manchu-Mongolian Language Parallels') in the *Proceedings of the Academy of Sciences of the USSR, Department of the Humanities*, 8–9: 1930, 601–26, 673–708; N. Poppe, *Introduction to Altaic Linguistics*, Wiesbaden: Harrassowitz, 1965, 161: 'The Mongolian influence on Manchu is so strong that a good knowledge of Mongolian is a prerequisite for successful study of Manchu'; Kyōko Maezono, *Verbbildungs-Suffixe in Mandschu und Mongolischen*, Wiesbaden: Harrassowitz, 2007 (esp. pp. 11, 173–75). See also W. Rozycki, *Mongol Elements in Manchu, UAS* 157, Bloomington: Indiana University RIFIAS, 1994.

7 The Mongolian translation (via Manchu) of the *Yuan History* (*Yuanshi*) was reprinted in one volume in Peking in 1987 (Dudang, Öljeitü et al., trans., *Dayiyuvan ulus-un teüke*). See the original 1664 introduction, *op. cit.*, 4–5.

title of the *Ocean of Stories* (*Üliger-ün dalai*).[8] This rich collection of narratives and the Geser epic were to become the two most popular and widely read works among the Mongols in the following centuries.

In the late 16th century, the Mongols had undergone a so-called 'second conversion' to Tibetan Buddhism — the 'first conversion' being ascribed to Khubilai Khan who, as is known, favoured Buddhism and the Tibetan clergy. There is no evidence, however, that Khubilai himself was a true and devout Buddhist.[9] It was the Altan Khan of the Tümed (r. 1542–82), one of the last rulers of the line of Genghis Khan (after the collapse of the Yuan dynasty in 1367) who, in 1577, formally converted to the Yellow Sect of Lamaism and installed the first Dalai Lama as head of the Buddhist Church in Tibet, conferring this title posthumously also to his two predecessors. Gradually, with the establishment of numerous monasteries and the spread of Buddhist teachings through itinerant monks and religious treatises, mostly printed in China, all the Mongols also converted to Lamaism. However, their native shamanism, mingled

8 See B. Laufer, '*Skizze der mongolischen Literatur*', *Keleti Szemle* 8:1907, 223–24; W. Heissig, *Die Pekinger*, 33 (27). Cf. J.W. De Jong, *Buddha's Word in China*, 28th George Ernest Morrison Lecture, The Australian National University, Canberra, 1968, 23–24, n. 39. A complete translation of the *Üliger-ün dalai* (1644 ed.) is found in S. Frye, tr., *The Sutra of the Wise and the Foolish* (*mdo bdzans blun*) *or The Ocean of Narratives (üliger-ün dalai)*, Library of Tibetan Works & Archives, Dharamsala, 1981.

9 There is plenty of evidence that Khubilai protected and actively promoted Buddhism, Lamaism in particular, and for that he is recognised by Tibetan and Mongol historiography as 'the wise Cakravarti King who turned the thousand golden wheels', hence his main epithet of Sečen Qan or Wise King. Cakravartin is an old Indian term for an (ideal) enlightened monarch under whom the entire world enjoys peace and justice. Cf., for example, I.J. Schmidt, tr., *Geschichte der Ost-Mongolen und ihres Fürstenhauses, verfasst von Ssanang Ssetsen Chungtaidschi der Ordus*, St Petersburg, Leipzig, 1829, 118–19. However, Khubilai's faith, and that of his court, was rather shallow and 'rested, in addition to the necessity for political instruction [through the regular appointment of Tibetan advisers as National Preceptors–I.R.], on the influence of Tibetan medicine as practiced by the Tibetan monks, which proved more convincing to the Mongols than the shamans' prayers for health and on the greater magical effectiveness of Tantric magic. Marco Polo reported that the monks of the Red Sect of Lamaism at the court of Khubilai vied with each other at feats of magic. Until the early 14th century, they were also competing in this field with the court shamans'. See W. Hessig, *The Religions of Mongolia*, tr. G. Samuel, London and Henley: Routledge & Kegan Paul, 1980, 24; Franke and Twitchett, eds, *op. cit.*, 457–62, 471–73. Tibet, as a subject and ally, had become part of the Mongol empire only a few years before Khubilai's self-enthronement; however, it was chronically divided by religious — largely monastic — rivalry and sectarian conflict. One of the main reasons for Khubilai's interest in Tibetan affairs was the internal pacification of this important border country and control over its troublesome people. This by no means easy task he tried to achieve by supporting the lamas of the leading Saskya sect, whose representative at the Mongol court in Ta-tu (Peking) was always a Saskya monk, like the earlier mentioned 'Phags-pa (see above, n. 3), Khubilai's first National Preceptor (*guoshi*). Cf. T.-T. Li, *The Historical Status of Tibet*, New York: King's Crown Press, Columbia University, 1956, 18–23; L. Petech, *Central Tibet and the Mongols. The Yüan-Sa-skya Period of Tibetan History*, Rome: Is.M.E.O., 1990, *passim*.

with the new faith, continued to be practised until modern times in the daily life of the population at large as a 'folk religion', alongside the formal Buddhist teaching of the monastic establishments.[10]

The folk religion of most people, besides the worship and appeasement of powerful deities representing forces of nature, also includes the cult of deified heroes and superhuman beings whose protection and help are sought on special occasions. This too applies to the Mongols of Mongolia, as well as to those who settled in north China — that is, the present-day Inner Mongolia Autonomous Region — from the 15th century on.[11] After the 'pacification' of Tibet in 1720, two years before the Kangxi emperor's death, and the submission of the northern (Khalkha) and western (Oirat) Mongols in 1691 and 1750 respectively, the Manchus, by the middle of the 18th century, had achieved their aim, although the resulting peace along the border remained unstable.[12] Furthermore, the Treaty of Kyakhta with Russia in 1727 had sanctioned Qing control over both Inner and Outer Mongolia.

In this period, the spread of Buddhism and of the Lamaist-influenced folk religion continued unabated, the former finding expression chiefly in the construction of well-endowed monasteries, and intense translation activity in cities such as Peking and Köke Qota,[13] resulting in the large-scale printing of sutras in Mongolian and Tibetan.[14] Folk religion, also largely spread among the Mongols of Inner Mongolia, had its 'centres' in the numerous shrines consecrated, among others, to the cult of a number of deities in the form of armed heroes on horseback whose main role was to protect the welfare of men, in particular by safeguarding their health and the herds of horses, guarding them from misfortune, ensuring good hunting and increasing their possessions, as well as assisting them in

10 See Heissig, *op. cit.*, 26ff. *et passim*; C.R. Bawden, *The Modern History of Mongolia*, London: Weidenfeld and Nicolson, 1968–26ff.

11 The modern region (est. 1947) of north China comprising the former provinces of Suiyuan, Chahar, Rehe (Jehol), Liaobei, and Xing'an, as well as the northern parts of Gansu and Ningxia. For the establishment of Mongol tribes south of the Gobi and their political separation from the Mongols north of the Gobi, leading to the creation of Outer (predominantly Khalkha) Mongolia and Inner (or Southern) Mongolia, see Bawden, *op. cit.*, ch. 2.

12 See L. Petech, *China and Tibet in the Early 18th Century: History of the Establishment of Chinese Protectorate in Tibet*, *T'oung Pao Monographie I*, Leiden: Brill, 1950; Li, *op. cit.*, ch. 3; Bawden, *op. cit.*, chs 2 and 3.

13 That is, present-day Huhhot ('Blue City'), the capital of Inner Mongolia built by Altan Khan, 'the first permanent Mongol city of modern times' (Bawden, *op. cit.*, 25).

14 See Heissig, *Die Pekinger* and, by the same author, *Die Familien- und Kirchengeschichtsschreibung der Mongolen, 1: 16–18 Jahrhundert*, *Asiat. Forschungen* 5, Wiesbaden: Harrassowitz, 1965; Bawden, *op. cit.*, 35–37.

times of warfare. One of the three major 'equestrian deities' worshipped by the Mongols with invocations and prayers, incense offerings, and other ritual acts was Geser Khan.[15]

Later in the Qing period, the cult of Geser Khan was associated with that of Guandi, the Chinese God of War, who was none other than Guan Yu (d. AD 219 or 220), the famous hero of the wars of the Three Kingdoms in the 3rd century AD, ennobled in the 12th century, then made a god in 1594 under emperor Shengzong (Wanli) of the Ming dynasty. This cultural assimilation of a 'Mongolised' Tibetan epic hero to a Chinese deified folk hero is an interesting phenomenon of acculturation in the folk religion and state cult of the Mongols and the Chinese through a Tibetan-Manchu medium, and has been discussed in detail by W. Heissig and others.[16]

One factor that fostered the fusion of the two martial deities was, undoubtedly, the fictionalised accounts of the *gesta* of the historical Guan Yu that made him one of the most popular figures in Chinese lore for his military prowess, courage, and unswerving loyalty. He was immortalised by Luo Guanzhong of the late Yuan – early Ming in his renowned *Romance of the Three Kingdoms* (*Sanguozhi tongsu yanyi*).[17] It is no coincidence that the Chinese title, as printed neatly on each folio of *Arban jüg-ün ejen Geser qaγan-u tuγuji orosiba* (*Story of King Geser, Lord of the Ten Quarters* (hereafter GK)), is *Sanguozhi* — an abbreviation of its full title. G. Roerich is, undoubtedly, right in surmising that an elegant blockprint edition of a popular Mongolian epic such as GK was part of the Manchus' policy of friendship towards the Mongolian people.[18] However, the addition of the title of a well-known Chinese romance

---

15 See Heissig, *The Religions of Mongolia*, 93–101.

16 *Ibid.*, 99ff.

17 The original Ming edition of the Hongzhi period (1488–1505) in 24 *juan* was first published in photo-reproduction by the Commercial Press, Shanghai, in 1929. A 24-*juan* edition of the *Romance* was translated into Manchu and printed in 1650. For a specimen of the printed Mongolian translation of the *Romance* see A. Pozdneev, ed., *Mongol'skaja khrestomatija dlja pervonachal'nago prepodavanija*, St Petersburg, 1900, 321–43. Cf. Heissig, *op. cit.*, 99, and H. Walravens, *Chinesische und manjurische Handschriften und seltene Drucke Teil 8: Mandschurische Handschriften und Drucke im Bestand der Staatsbibliothek zu Berlin*, Stuttgart: Steiner, 2014, no. 59 (pp. 137–39). As in the case of the Manchu translation of the Liao, Jin, and Yuan Imperial Annals, the Mongolian version of the *Romance* was done from the Manchu, not from the Chinese.

18 See Heissig, *op. cit.*, 99, 125, n. 387. Cf. R.A. Stein, *L'épopée tibétaine de Gesar dans sa version lamaïque de Ling*, Paris: PUF, 1956, Introduction, 1: 'En mongol, une seule version imprimée, publiée à Pékin en 1716, doit son existence au souci de la dynastie mandchoue de se ménager les Tibétains et les Mongols en adoptant le héros Gesar comme dieu tutélaire de la dynastie et en l'assimilant au dieu chinois de la guerre, Kouan-ti'.

extolling the personality and deeds of a native folk hero who by 1716 had been (for well over a century!) elevated to the rank of God of War, indicates more than a general similitude between two epic novels, one Mongolian of Tibetan origin, the other Chinese. It alludes and preludes, in my opinion, to a strong correlation between the two main heroes, *viz.* Geser Khan, Lord of the Ten Quarters, and Guandi, God of War, destined eventually to be fused into a single entity, Vaiśravana, the Lamaist god lCam-sring, a warrior deity and guardian of wealth.[19] This process of assimilation, which is of common occurrence with the gods and goddesses of ancient civilisations (Indo-Iranian, Greco-Roman, etc.), took its time, and it was not completed until the middle of the 19th century, by which time Guandi and Geser Khan were equated in worship in temples scattered throughout the Qing empire, with Guandi — hence Geser — well established as the tutelary deity of the dynasty. Some cities, such as Uliasutai in west central Mongolia, became famous for their temple of Geser Khan. It must be said, however, that matters of Lamaist theology and state cult were not of much concern to the population in general. Heissig writes:

> For the Mongolian people on the other hand, Geser Khan remained the equestrian warrior-god, with traits taken from the folk epic. The syncretic arrangements remained without deeper effect. Occasionally, it is true, the title of a copy of an older Geser Khan prayer would now give the name of Kuan-ti in place of that of Geser Khan, without otherwise altering the previous wording; the Mongols regarded the Kuan-ti statues in the temples of the Manchu state god and god of war as representations of their beloved hero Geser Khan ... In his role of protective deity of the Mongols, guarding against harm to the flocks, from weather and from illness, the Geser Khan of the Mongolian Geser Khan epic continued to be worshipped up until the 1930s, at least among the East Mongolian tribes ... The Geser Khan epic was widely distributed in many impressions from the 1716 blockprint edition and in beautiful manuscripts agreeing with the printed version. On

19 That is, the Mongolian Bisman Tngri; this god is a late Mongol adoption from the Buddhist pantheon. See Heissig, *op. cit.*, Index, s.vv. Bisman Tngri and Vaiśravana. When in the early 19th century Guandi was included into the Lamaist pantheon by the Lamaist Church, Guandi was equated with Vaiśravana with whom Geser Khan had already been identified in Tibet. See *ibid.*, 100. The ancient Indian god Vaiśravana was originally a king of evil spirits who became a god of wealth (like the Roman Pluto) and, as one of the four Mahārājas, he is a guardian at the entrance of Buddhist temples. See W.E. Soothill and L. Hodous, *A Dictionary of Chinese Buddhist Terms with Sanskrit and English Equivalents and a Sanskrit-Pali Index*, London: K. Paul, Trench, Trubner, 1937, 306a–b.

occasions of illness, threatening danger and sickness in the herds, parts of the epic were recited by Lamaist monks. The texts of the epic were treated with great respect, and had always to be kept in a horizontal position in a 'pure' place, in order not to anger Geser Khan.[20]

The Tibetan Epic of King Gesar

The epic cycle of King Gesar (*ge sar rgyal po* in Tibetan)[21] is the national epos of Tibet and one of the great epics of the world's oral literature. Sung by itinerant bards in poetry or in a mixture of prose and poetry in Tibet, and in several neighbouring countries of Central Asia and northern India over many centuries, the epic was continually enriched and diversified, and its various versions were recorded in writing. Manuscript copies proliferated until printed editions finally appeared in recent times.

Having gained Baltistan and Ladakh in the southwest, the epic penetrated into Nepal, Sikkim, and Bhutan. Tibetan bards also spread it among the Sino-Tibetan tribes of western Yunnan. In the northeast, through China (Inner Mongolia) and Mongolia, it reached Manchuria and Siberia, where, with the *J̌anggar*, it become a favourite Buriat epic. In the north and northwest, it reached the Uighurs and the Oirat Mongols. We have long and short versions, in Tibetan and its dialects as well as in Mongolian, Buriat, and Kalmyk. It is still sung and expanded today in Inner Mongolia, one of the latest version by the great contemporary bard Pajai (1902–62) being many tens of thousands

20 See Heissig, *op. cit.*, 101. Cf. also V. Veit. 'Some marginal notes on Geser Khan in Mongol tradition', in K. Kollmar-Paulenz, C. Peter, eds, *Tractata Tibetica et Mongolica. Festschrift für Klaus Sagaster zum 65. Geburtstag, Asiat. Forschungen* 145, Wiesbaden: Harrassowitz, 2002, 299–304.

21 The name of the epic's hero, Gesar, is not Tibetan but the transcription of the Greek title *kaisar* 'king, emperor', which became known to the Tibetans through the intermediary of the Turks of Central Asia in the 9th and 10th centuries. Always, according to R.A. Stein, the fuller name designation of 'Gesar of Khrom (or better Phrom)' of the Tibetan epic 'represents Frūm, an Iranian form of the name Rūm that is Eastern Rome (Byzance) and Turkish Anatolia'. See the English Introduction to *The Epic of Gesar* published by Kunzang Tobgyel, vol. 1, Thimphu, Bhutan: Jayyed Press, 1979, 19; R.-A. Stein, *Recherches sur l'épopée et le barde au Tibet*, Paris: PUF, 1959, 279–99. Stein, *loc. cit.*, also connects the name-title of Kaisar/Gesar with the Indian notion of *cakravatin*, that is, of a world's monarch who establishes justice and peace, and the related concepts of subduer of enemies, leader of armies, master of wealth, protector-king, etc., inherited from ancient legends and myths concerning the great conquerors and rulers of the past (Alexander, Aśoka, Kaniṣka) later grafted to the figure and mission of the legendary Gesar. Blending these heterogeneous elements borrowed from local folklore with Lamaist culture was the work — the 'singing and narrating' — of centuries in different localities, making use of both the oral medium and the written (= manuscript) tradition handed down by professional bards.

of verses long. Here lies, of course, the difference between the cycle of Gesar/Geser and the great Indian and Greek epics, the former being still productive and open to additions and variations, while the latter are static, immutable and fixed in time.

Manuscripts of the numerous Tibetan oral versions are scattered in libraries and private collections all over the world and some of these have been published. Of the printed versions, one should mention the three-volume edition known as the Ling blockprint (from Gling-chang, the place of publication)[22] of the second half of the 19th century; the Gyangtze blockprint in 10 chapters, undated but compiled (not printed) before the beginning of the 18th century;[23] and the long Bhutanese version, published in Thimphu by Kunzang Tobgyel (1979).[24] A Chinese compilation containing all the Tibetan versions is being prepared.[25]

Except perhaps for one, Tibetan printed editions are comparatively modern. Thus, the earliest dated printed edition of the epic is actually the Mongolian version of 1716, issued in Peking, which will be discussed further on in more detail.

No single manuscript or printed edition contains the entire text of the Tibetan saga that may ultimately consist of 29 chapters altogether.[26] They usually contain a single chapter, the one that the bards learned and sang, that is their individual repertory. Some were more popular than others (as with the arias of Western operas), and the listeners also

22 Present-day Lingcang in eastern Tibet. This was the old kingdom of Khams established between the towns of Jyekundo and Dajianlu where Gesar, according to a local (and widely accepted) tradition, is deemed to hail from, although other areas of Tibet claimed this honour. Therefore, Gesar is often referred to as 'Gesar of Ling', usually followed by several other glorifying epithets such as Best of Beings, Jewel, and Conqueror of Enemies. A shortened French translation of the Ling blockprint edition, preceded by an important introduction is found in Stein, *L'épopée*. In *Recherches* the same author gives a critical list of the extant oral and written (manuscripts, blockprints, and books) versions of the Gesar epic in Tibetan and Mongolian (56–106).

23 See Stein, *Recherches*, 67–71.

24 See above, n. 21. There are also xylographs of individual chapters and prayers or invocations to Gesar, all listed by Stein.

25 See L. Harvilahti, 'Epos and National Identity: Transformations and Incarnations', *Oral Tradition* (Peking) 11: 1996, 42.

26 The number of chapters has progressively changed over the years. The Chinese compilation (see above, n. 25) divides the *corpus gesaricus* of Tibetan versions into 29 chapters. Cf. *Recherches*, 43–55, which gives a maximum total of 25 chapters, which corresponds to the number given by Žamcarano for the longest Mongolian version known, but unfortunately lost.

learned them by heart, and this till not long ago. The 'stories' of Gesar and his legendary feats were recited often to the accompaniment of a 'horse-head fiddle' or a drum with bells according to the circumstances.[27]

The story of Gesar is the following, as one can extrapolate it from the Tibetan versions, which, we must emphasise, vary a good deal among themselves not only in the details but also in the presence or absence of religious, that is Buddhist, motifs and the like. At the beginning — as a prelude — the world was in a state of chaos, dominated by violent rulers assisted by demons and evil spirits. Tibet is the centre of the world. The legend relates how the country is converted to Buddhism by the great teacher Padmasambhava, and how the latter convokes an assembly of the gods and Buddhas to avert the danger of the destruction of religion on earth posed by a woman who vows to be reborn as a devil. Her curse would, in fact, materialise with the birth of the three Hor demon-kings, sworn enemies of Buddhism. Hence the assembly's decision to send one of the gods, the future King Gesar, down to earth to destroy the demon-kings and their kingdoms, protect the dharma, and become lord of the world.

The designated god is, thus, miraculously born on earth.[28] He is ugly and gauche, and is named Joro.[29] However, as a divine incarnation, he is endowed with magical powers. Thanks to these powers, he establishes himself, eventually winning a race against many odds, the prize of which is the throne of Ling. As king, Joru drops his ordinary name and becomes Gesar. His first wife is 'Brug-mo. He has also a vile old uncle called Khro-thung who hates him and tries to kill him and possess his wife. King Gesar now embarks on his divine mission, the first task of which is to destroy the enemies of Buddhism, the evil rulers and the powerful demons. He begins his campaign by going to China where the emperor's wife is a Buddhism-hating demon. He also has problems with the emperor's five daughters, who are all incarnations of the goddess Tārā. With his magic power, he overcomes all his enemies in that land and restores Buddhism. Next, and through several colourful adventures

27 The distinction between professional bards, often performing in temples, and itinerant and amateur ones, as well as the different types and styles of the recitals (with musical accompaniment and without), the dress of the bards and the religious character of the same, the events (marriages, festivals, etc.) requiring these performances, and many other matters concerning them are discussed in ch. 7 of *Recherches*. For the characteristic fiddle of Mongolian origin, see *op.cit.*, 379.

28 Different versions give different accounts on how Gesar was born and who his mother and father were.

29 Meaning 'bastard, natural son'. According to one version, he was the son of a slave and the king of Ling.

and reverses, Gesar destroys the three kings of Hor, incarnations of the woman who had made the vow to suppress Buddhism in Tibet. There follow more conquests and submissions of kings and kingdoms in the south, in Iran, in Mongolia and further north. Gesar is also interested in the quest for precious stones, pearls, and exotic and rare objects. It is in search of these that he travels to Kashmir and beyond India. He goes to Nepal and obtains its submission too. After a further quest for a precious 'pearl with nine eyes', crowned with success, Gesar descends to Hell to rescue his mother.

The above résumé is only a brief excursus of the main episodes; it is by no means complete even within the confines of the Tibetan corpus and does not include the many episodes described in the Mongolian version, which are not found in any other version. For further details, the reader is directed to the lists of events and the analysis of the same provided by the late Professor R. Stein.[30]

As for the translations of the Tibetan Gesar epos into Western languages, they are all partial versions as no translation of the 'entire' epic is possible at this stage because of the sheer size of what has been handed down and the fact that some chapters are apparently lost, most likely forever.[31]

The abridged French translation of the three volumes (out of nine) of the Ling blockprint edition has already been mentioned.[32]

In German, there are three versions of Gesar stories recited mostly in the Ladakhi dialect, and collected and translated by A.H. Francke, a prolific Gesar scholar and author of several important studies on the subject.[33] His major work on the Lower Ladhakhi version has also appeared in English.[34]

A version of the epic from Amdo in northeastern Tibet (Q̱inghai) was translated into German by M. Hermanns.[35]

---

30 *Recherches*, 42–55. Cf. also the numerous references to the various episodes in the Tibetan and other versions — especially the Mongolian ones — in ch. 10. The volume of *Recherches* is still the most valuable tool and guide for the study of all the aspects of the Gesar epic.

31 Stein, *Recherches*, 43, 45; *L'épopée*, 2–3, 5.

32 See above, n. 22.

33 See Stein, *Recherches*, 12–14, 56–57.

34 A.H. Francke, *A Lower Ladakhi Version of the Kesar Saga. Bibliotheca Indica* 1543, Calcutta, 1941. Cf. Stein, *Recherches*, 13.

35 M. Hermanns, tr., *Das National-Epos der Tibeter Gling König Ge Sar*, Regensburg: J. Habbel Verlag, 1965. Hermanns claims that the Gesar epic pre-dates Buddhism in Tibet and is a product of the nomadic culture of northeastern Tibet.

In English, the 1933 translation by A. David-Neel and the Lama Yongden (originally published in French) made the Tibetan epic known to the English-speaking public.[36] It was revised and reissued in 1959, with an informative introduction (34 pages). The translation (some 225 pages) is a summarised mixture of several Gesar stories collected in eastern Tibet and presented in narrative form.[37]

The Tibetan cycle of Gesar is, of course, referred to in the many works — books and articles — on the Mongolian version of the epic to which we shall now turn.

The Mongolian Epic of Geser Khan

The seven books or chapters (*bölög*) of the 1716 Mongolian blockprint are regarded as the *editio princeps* of the epic; but it is not only the first printed edition, it is also the text edition first reprinted in Europe and translated into a Western language.[38] The merit for this remarkable achievement for its time goes to the Dutch scholar I.J. Schmidt (1779–1847), well-known author of the first scientific grammar of Written Mongolian and the first Mongolian dictionary, and the translator of the New Testament into Mongolian (Kalmyk and literary) and of Saγang Sečen's chronicle *Erdeni-yin tobči* (*Precious Summary*) from the Mongolian into German.

36 A. David-Neel and the Lama Yongden, *The Superhuman Life of Gesar of Ling*, translated with the collaboration of V. Sydney, London: Rider & Company, 1933, rev. ed., 1959.

37 For a critical appraisal see Stein, *Recherches*, 57–58. For a more scholarly English translation of a few chapters of a Tibetan version see R. Brooks Kornman, *A Comparative Study of a Buddhist Version of the Epic of Gesar of Ling*, PhD dissertation, Princeton University, 1994, Ann Arbor: UMI Dissertation Services, 1997.

38 I.J. Schmidt, ed., *Die Thaten des Vertilgers der zehn Übel in den zehn Gegenden des verdienstvollen Helden Bogda Gesser Chan; eine mongolische Heldensage, nach einem in Peking gedruckten Exemplare aufs Neue abgedruckt unter der Aufsicht des Akademikers I.J. Schmidt*, St Petersburg: Kaiserl. Akad. der Wiss.,1836, repr. Osnabrück: O. Zeller, 1965 (Mongolian text); I.J. Schmidt, tr., *Die Thaten Bogda Gesser Chan's, des Vertilgers der Wurzel der zehn Übel in den zehn Gegenden. Eine ostasiatische Heldensage aus dem mongolischen übersetz*, St Petersburg: Kaiserl. Akad. der Wiss., 1839, repr. Berlin: Auriga, 1925, and Osnabrück: O. Zeller, 1966 (translation). See H. Walravens, *Isaac Jakob Schmidt (1779–1847). Leben und Werk des Pioniers der mongolischen und tibetischen Studien. Eine Dokumentation, Abh. für die Kunde des Morgenlandes* 56, 1, Wiesbaden: Harrassowitz, 2005, 63–69, nos 48, 49. See also his other contributions to Mongolian and Tibetan studies cited in the volume.

About 100 years after the publication of Schmidt's translation of GK, the Russian Mongolist S.A. Kozin published his translation of the same text. Although he corrects some faulty renderings of Schmidt, his overall translation is not as good as the former's.[39]

The Mongolian text of the 1716 blockprint[40] is written in a language that is different in many respects from written Mongolian and betrays a southern, that is, Inner Mongolian, dialect of the 17th–18th centuries. This was first pointed out in 1926 by N. Poppe, who, after a thorough analysis of its grammatical features, came to the conclusion that 'the language of the Gesserkhan is a mixture of a South Mongolian dialect and the literary language'.[41] We are dealing, it seems, with a dialect close to the Ordos and Ǖjümüčin dialects as well as to Monguor, which tally with the tradition that the Mongol saga of Geser originates from the area of Qinghai (Kokonor and western Gansu) among the Mongol-speaking ethnic groups who had settled there.[42] Thus while the cradle of the story is northeastern Tibet, when spreading north and northeast beyond the Tibetan cultural domain it acquired a Mongol character and a life of its own, retaining at the same time the main thematic features

39 S.A. Kozin, tr., *Geseriada. Skazanie o milostivom Geser Mergen-Khane iskorenitele desjati zol v desjati stranakh sveta*, Moscow-Leningrad: Izd. Akad. Nauk SSSR, 1935. See N. Poppe, 'Stand und Aufgaben der Mongolistik', *Zeitschrift des Deutchen Morgenländischen Gesellschaft* 100:1950, 82–83.

40 The blockprint consists of 177 folios divided into seven books or chapters (52+5+12 +27+60+7+5=177) with 25 lines of text per page, hence 50 in each folio. Except for ch. 1, 2a, which has only 19 lines. Each chapter is individually numbered in both Mongolian and Chinese. (The Chinese title *Sanguo zhi* on each page has already been discussed). The size of the blockprint is 56x18cm (text: 46x13cm). There are illustrations on the first page on both sides of the text, which has only eight lines, representing on the left the god Qormusda on an elephant with two attendants, on the right Geser Khan on a horse with two warriors. On the last page there is the image of a group of four personages (Geser, Jasa Šikir, and two others) each with two attendants. The colophon on ch. 7, 5a, gives the date corresponding to 'an auspicious day of the first month' (24 January – 22 February) 1716 preceded by a title of the work longer than the one on the first page (see above, n. 1). See Stein, *Recherches*, 75–76, 104, n. 92.

41 Poppe's masterful article on the language of GK, 'Geserica. Untersuchung der sprachlichen Eigen-tümlichkeiten der mongolischen Version des Gesserkhan', appeared in *Asia Major* 3: 1926, 1–32 and 167–93. The passage cited is on page 192. See also below, n. 42f.

42 Cf. G. Kara, *Chants d'un barde mongol*, *Bibl. Orient. Hung.* 12, Budapest: Akadémiai Kiadó, 1970, 208–209. For the language peculiarities of GK, see also H.-P. Vietze, 'Zur Sprache der Pekinger Version der Geser-Sage', in W. Heissig, ed., *Fragen der mongolischen Heldendichtung*, III: Vorträge des 4. Epensymposiums des Sonderforschungsbereichs 12, Bonn, 1982, *Asiat. Forschungen* 91, Wiesbaden: Harrassowitz, 1985, 549–54. Vietze also agrees with the southwestern nature of the Mongolian dialect of the GK. As is known, A. Bobrovnikov's *Grammatika mongol'sko-kalmyckago jazyka* (Kazan', 1849) describes the language of the GK in the mistaken belief that it was literary Mongolian.

and *dramatis personae* of the Tibetan cycle.[43] In short, we are dealing with a Mongolian *rifacimento* (with many additional episodes) of a Tibetan epic that has its roots in that country's Lamaist culture. Nevertheless, the discovery of some fragments of manuscripts concerning the Mongol epic and two complete texts (an incense offering and a prayer to Geser), all dating from the beginning of the 17th century, indicate beyond doubt that our hero and his deeds were known to the Mongols at least a century before the Peking blockprint edition.[44] One may, indeed, postulate that the beginning of the elaboration of the Mongolian Geser cycle coincides broadly with the second conversion of the Mongols to Buddhism, that is, the end of the 16th century.

So far, we have dealt with the Peking blockprint edition in seven chapters. We do not know the circumstances of its composition, but the printed text of 1716 no doubt rests on an oral tradition. We have, in fact, various manuscripts, that is, manuscript copies, of the Geser stories in GK with interesting variants, but all more or less contemporary with GK, although some scholars claim that the original of one of them goes back to the first half of the 17th century.[45] Several of these manuscript copies have been described by Stein, who also reviews Oirat and Buriat versions of the epic.[46] The investigation and publication of these manuscripts in the Soviet Union, Mongolia, and China in the second half of the 20th century led to further research on the Geser epic in various other countries, such as Germany and Hungary, resulting in the

43 See Ts. Damdinsuren, 'On the new edition of the Mongolian version "Geseriada"', in W. Heissig, ed., *op. cit.*, 593–99; L. Ligeti, 'Un episode d'origine chinoise du "Geser-qan"', *Acta Orientalia Hung.* 1: 1950, 340–43; C. Damdinsuren, 'Explanation of some personal names in Mongolian epos about Geser', in W. Heissig, *Fragen der mongolisch Heldendichtung*, IV: Vorträge des 5. Epensymposiums des Sonderforschungsbereichs 12, Bonn 1985, *Asiat. Forschungen* 101, Wiesbaden: Harrassowitz, 1987, 375–80.

44 See Kara, *Chants*, 209; E. Chiodo, *The Mongolian Manuscripts on Birch Bark from Xarbuxyn Balgas in the Collection of the Mongolian Academy of Sciences*, Part 1, *Asiat. Forschungen* 137, Wiesbaden: Harrassowitz, 2000, 148–49 and 164–68 (mss. XBM 66 & XBM 73). Cf. W. Heissig, 'Zu einigen Textvarianten des mongolischen Geser-Rauchopfers', in K. Kollmar-Paulenz, C. Peter, eds, *Tractata Tibetica et Mongolica*, 103–18.

45 This is the so-called Nomči Qatun's version of GK, which was published for the first time in two volumes in Ulan Bator in 1960 (*Corpus Scriptorum Mongolorum* 9, fasc. 4 and 4a), together with the Caya version (*CSM* 9, fasc. 2 and 2a). See below, nn. 47 and 49. Although in many respects superior to the 1716 edition, and therefore of great help in reading GK, these two manuscript copies are roughly contemporary with the former. See C. Damdinsuren, *Istoričeskije korni Geseriady*, Moscow: Izd. ANSSSR, 1957, 61ff. (note, however, that on page 56, D. mentions a Mongol tradition according to which GK was first recorded about 1630 by five Oirat bards of the Kokonor region), and by the same author, 'On the new edition', 598–99; cf. Kara, *Chants*, 209 and n. 379; U. Secenmunkh, *Issledovanie pis'mennogo mongol'skogo eposa o Gesere*, St Petersburg, 2004, 142, 233; and Heissig, 'Zu einigen Textvarianten', 104.

46 Stein, *Recherches*, 60ff., 92ff.

identification of several more chapters of the epic previously unknown. In 1927, N. Poppe had announced the discovery of seven 'new' chapters, representing chapters 8, 9, 10, 12, 13, 14, and 15, as the continuation of GK. In the early 1950s, W. Heissig found, in Belgium, two more songs corresponding to chapters 8, 9, and 10. In 1956, an important Chinese edition of the epic was published in two volumes, the first one containing the text of GK, and the second that of six additional chapters (8–13), which, according to Heissig, actually correspond to chapters 8, 9, 10a, 10b, 11, 13, 14, and 16/17. In 1960, in the series *Corpus scriptorum mongolorum* (*CSM*) of the MPR Academy of Sciences, several manuscript copies of Mongolian versions of the epic (some just variants of GK) and an Oirat version were published in facsimile under the editorship of B. Rintchen. The interrelation between the 'old' seven chapters of GK and the 'new' chapters, with their similitudes, repetitions, and analogical episodes recurring in different chapters, have been analysed over the years by Damdinsuren, Heissig, and others. Themes and logical sequences were duly taken into account.[47] Unfortunately, on a subject like the open, evolving saga of Geser, subject to all sorts of variations by individual bards and storytellers, nothing is clear-cut and scholars have reached different conclusions. For Damdisuren, the Mongolian cycle, as it can be established on the evidence of the sources available at present, consists of 12 chapters (seven of the GK plus five 'new' ones), but these can actually be reduced to nine because three (chapters 10, 11, and 12) are similar to chapters 4 and 5, and the episodes described in Chapter 12 are 'depicted' in the other chapters. For Heissig, on the other hand, the 'new' chapters are eight (chapters 8, 9, 10a, 10 [15], 11, 13, 14, 16/17).[48]

47 On all these questions, see N. Poppe, 'Stand und Aufgaben der Mongolistik', 83; W. Heissig, *A Lost Civilization. The Mongols Rediscovered*, tr. by D.J.S. Thomson, London: Thames and Hudson, 1966, 134–51; *Arban Jug-ün eǰen Geser qaγan-u tuγuǰi orosiba*, I–II, Peking-Kökeqota: Öbör Mongγol-un arad-un keblel-ün qoriya, 1956; Rintchen, ed., *Nomči qatun's Version of Kesar Saga* I, *CSM* 9: 1960, fasc. 4; *idem* II, *CSM* 9: 1960, fasc. 4a; *Caya's Version of Kesar Saga* I, *CSM* 9: 1960, fasc. 2; *idem* II, *CSM* 9: 1960, fasc. 2a; *Žamcarano's Version of Kesar Saga* I, *CSM* 9: 1960, fasc. 3a; *idem* II, *CSM* 9: 1960, fasc. 3b; *Version oirate des chansons de Guesser* I–II: *CSM* 9: 1960, fasc. 1; *Camling Senčin-ü namtar orosiba*, *CSM* 10: 1959; and, above all, W. Heissig, *Geser-Studien. Untersuchungen zu den Erzählstoffen in den 'neuen' Kapiteln des mongolischen Geser-Zyklus*, Opladen: Westdeutscher Verlag, 1983, as well the numerous volumes of *Acts of the Bonn Symposia on the Mongolian Epic* edited by W. Heissig and published in the series *Asiatische Forschungen*.

48 Cf. Damdinsuren's 'On the new edition', 597, and Heissig, *Geser-Studien*, 7–8, 21–228. Stein, *Recherches*, 94, breaks down the new chapters in vol. 2 of the 1956 Peking-Kökeqota edition as follows: ch. 1: Geser's heroes (= ch. 8); ch. 2 (= ch. 9, Angdulman); ch. 3 (var. of ch. 6, Lubsaga); ch. 4 (= ch. 10, Saixulai Goa); ch. 5 (= ch. 12, Gümbü-xan); ch. 6 (= ch. 13, Način-xan of the North). The correspondences are with the Khalkha manuscript version discovered by Žamcarano (*Recherches*, 94 [50]). Cf. above, n. 47.

An indispensable tool for the study of the Mongolian cycle of Geser is the *corpus gesericus*, currently being published in 12 volumes in Peking under the general editorship of Professor Sechenmöngke: *Geser-ün bürin bičig. A Complete Edition of Mongolian Geser*, Peking: Ündüsüten-ü keblel-ün qoriya, 2002– .[49]

In this project, we intended to deal only with the seven chapters of GK. They are of uneven length and their contents can be summarised as follows:

Chapter 1: Council of the gods to send a son of Qormusda Tengri (= the Indian god Indra) to earth to fight evil demons and ruthless humans, and establish peace, thus saving mankind by ruling over it like a Cakravartin King. Qormusda's youngest son accepts the task and is born as Joro (Joru), the future Geser (Gesar), Lord of the Ten Quarters. His youth is spent as a physically unattractive boy endowed with superhuman powers, and a regular prankster always in conflict with his evil uncle Čotong and his envious brother Rongsa. He fights ogres and demons and foils many attempts on his life. Still a teenager, Joro wins and marries the beautiful Rogmo in spite of Čotong's many attempts to take her for himself. He assumes the name Geser. Romantic interlude with Aǰu Mergen, daughter of the king of the dragons.

49 Professor Sechenmöngke of the Institute of Literature, Chinese Academy of Social Sciences (CASS), has been researching the Geser epic for many years. The *Geser-ün bürin bičig*, vol. 1, is entirely dedicated to the GK *plenior*, that is, the seven chapters of the 1716 edition plus the six additional chapters included in vol. 2 of the 1956 Peking-Kökeqota edition (see above, n. 47) of which the editor gives: 1. the full text transcribed in modern standard Mongolian script or *uyiγurǰin*; 2. the romanised transcription; 3. the photo-reproduction of the original texts; 4. 1,268 notes to 1. This volume thus replaces the often faulty 1956 Peking-Kökeqota edition, but one must continually check the transcriptions (especially 2.) against the facsimile of the text. Vol. 5 (2008), 1243–1325, contains the Oirat version of GK with the *todo* script of the Oirats turned into *uyiγurǰin*. Vol. 6 (2009): 1. 1–293, contains the text, transcribed into *uyiγurǰin*, of the *Nomči qatun-u Geser-ün tuγuǰi*; followed by 2. the *Caya-yin Geser-ün tuγuǰi* (299–627); 3. the romanised transcription of 1. (759–1051); 4. the romanised transcription of 2. (1057–1404); 5. a photo-reproduction of the manuscript of 1. (1415–1574); 6. a photo-reproduction of 2. (1577–1839). The above are some of the most important versions of the Mongolian text of particular usefulness in the translation of GK. In this connection one should mention also the two-volume edition of Y. Čimeddorǰi, *Geser Qaγan-u tuγuǰi*, Kökeqota: Öbör Mongγol-un arad-un keblel-ün qoriya, 1985, in 16 chapters (seven plus nine additional ones), which is a conflation of several versions to produce a more coherent narrative in more or less logical sequence. It contains numerous annotations that, combined with those of Sechenmöngke's edition, are of much help in understanding many difficult passages. For GK, one must take into account also the posthumous work in Cyrillic prepared by the great Mongol scholar C. Damdinsuren edited by Š. Gaadamba entitled *Geser*, Ulan Bator: Academy of Sciences of the Mongolian People's Republic, 1986, a valuable revised edition of the 1716 version with numerous interpolations in square brackets from other versions and modern equivalents, in round brackets, of obsolete terms.

Chapter 2: This brief chapter describes Geser's defeat, with the help of his good brother J̌asa Šikir and his 30 companions, of an ogre (*mangγus/ manggus*) who has transformed himself into a colossal black-striped tiger. After an epic fight with the ogre, they kill him and out of his skin and fur fashion various articles (helmets and shields).

Chapter 3: Geser's journey to China (Kitad) to assume control of the country whose ruler, Güme Qaγan, is in deep mourning following his wife's death and is unable to conduct affairs of state. Geser buries the empress, soothes the emperor, and brings order to the administration. Before returning home, he takes Güme Qaγan's daughter Güne Γooa as his wife.

Chapter 4: Geser is ill and his evil uncle Čotong and his principal wife Rogmo put the blame on Aralγa Γooa (the Arulγa Γooa of Chapter 1), now also a wife of Geser known as Tümen J̌irγalang ('Myriad Joys'), and banish her to the north, where, in despair, she marries a 12-headed ogre. Geser travels north, fights and kills the *mangγus*, seizes the country and settles there for nine years. Aralγa gives him a magic potion that makes him forget all about his past.

Chapter 5: This chapter is entirely taken by the war with the country of Sirayiγol (= Šaraiγol), that is, the country of Hor of the Tibetan version[50] and its kings, involving also Čotong, as usual up to no good, Rogmo Γooa, all Geser's companions, and his brother J̌asa Šikir, who are killed one by one. Eventually Geser, who frees himself at last from the bewitching effect of the potion of forgetfulness, returns home. He punishes Čotong and penetrates into the Šaraiγol territory, defeats its three kings and rescues Rogmo Γooa.

Chapter 6: An ogre in the guise of a lama captivates Geser's wife Rogmo, who persuades Geser to receive the lama's consecration. Thereupon Geser is magically turned into an ass, which the *mangγus*-lama takes to his home and uses for grinding flour. He also seizes Rogmo Γooa. Another wife of Geser's, AJ̌u Mergen (first met in Chapter 1), deceives the false lama and takes away the ass. Then, by means of a holy drink, Qormusda Tengri restores Geser's human form. The *mangγus*-lama is promptly killed by Geser, who takes Rogmo home, punishes her, and shows his gratitude to AJ̌u Mergen.

50 See the numerous references in Stein, *Recherches*, 601a, s.v.

Chapter 7: Geser finds out that his mother (Sanglun's wife) Gegše Amurčila is dead and has gone to Hell (*tamu*). He immediately follows her to the underworld. He punishes Erlig Qaγan, the ruler of the underworld, for having unjustly placed her there. She is released and reborn in Heaven, in the land of bliss.

While the seven chapters of GK are suffused with Lamaist culture, this is not the predominant influence in the Mongolian narrative, which relies more on the profane, entertaining value of semicomic human-like situations, flavoured with tricks, deception, magic, and picaresque interludes, the emphasis being on the bizarre, unusual, and unexpected. The 'new' chapters included in vol. 2 of the 1956 Peking-Kökeqota edition are, on the other hand, strongly influenced by Lamaist culture and in general less 'entertaining' than the episodes in GK. For a summary of the contents of these additional chapters, the interested reader can turn to the already mentioned works by Damdinsuren and Heissig.[51] In any event, there is no foundation in the claim, sometimes made in the past, that the new chapters, more so than the standard seven, reflect the popular opposition to the oppressive regime of the Mongol nobles and the lamas.[52]

Within the limited scope of this introduction, we cannot deal with the rich fields of Oirat, Buriat, and Khalkha epics;[53] however, we must say something about the translations of the GK into other languages and about the present version.

51 Damdinsuren, 'On the new edition', 595–97; Heissig, *Geser-Studien*, 8.

52 Cf. C.R. Bawden, *Letteratura mongola*. Estratto dalla *Storia delle letterature d'Oriente* diretta da Oscar Botto, Milano: Vallardi, 1969, 356.

53 The Oirat, Buriat, and Khalkha versions of the Geser epic are touched upon also by Stein in *Recherches*, 60–64, 93–94. Many important contributions on the subject (including translations) were published in Russian and German by N. Poppe, as well as by Russian, Kalmyk, Buriat, and Mongol scholars past and present like C. Žamcarano, B. Rintchen, S. Nekljudov, Ž. Tumurčeren, T. Basangovoj, B. Okonov, E. Mučkinova, G. Šarakšinova, A. Sakharovska, V. Soloukhin, and many others.

The German version by I.J. Schmidt of 1839 and the Russian one by S.A. Kozin of 1935 have already been mentioned.[54] Together with B. Bergmann's shorter version of two chapters of the GK,[55] Schmidt's translation of the GK served as the basis for I. Zeitlin's *Gessar Khan*, the story retold in English, very freely and selectively, for the general public and published in New York in 1927.[56] Zeitlin's work was, in turn, 'adapted' for another popular edition published in Berkeley, California, in 1991.[57] None of these versions renders the poetical passage in the GK in verse form.[58]

In 1962, W. Heissig published a German translation of the two 'songs' on Geser that he had found a few years earlier in Belgium (see above), corresponding to chapters 8, 9, and 10 of the 1956 Peking-Kökeqota edition (vol. 2, 1–52).[59] Two further chapters, this time both from the GK (chapters 3 and 6) were translated into English by C.R. Bawden and published in 2003 in his rich *Anthology*.[60]

For readers who know Hungarian well there is an interesting and original version in that language (with plenty of argot!) by the well-known contemporary Mongolist and writer L. Lőrincz, published in Budapest in 1982.[61]

Chinese, Japanese, and Korean scholars have also been active in translating the GK into their respective languages. In 1985 and 1989, two modern Chinese versions appeared in China, both translations

54 See also above, nn. 38 and 39.

55 B. Bergmann, *Nomadische Streifereien unter den Kalmüken in den Jahren 1802 und 1803*, vol. 3, Riga, 1804, 233–84.

56 *Gessar Khan*. Told by Ida Zeitlin, illustrated by Theodore Nadejen, New York: G.H. Doran, 1927.

57 *Gesar! The Wondrous Adventures of King Gesar*, adapted by Z. Wallace, illustrations by J. Witwer, Berkeley: Dharma Publishing, 1991. The cover title is, however, *Gesar! The Epic Tale of Tibet's Great Warrior-King*. See the review by K. Hitchins in *Central Asiatic Journal* 38: 1994, 113.

58 The GK is a mixture of prose and alliterative poetry. The latter is used 1. for citations of short sayings and proverbs, and 2. for longer passages that require declaiming or singing; however, very often the 'poetical' value of such passages is not apparent in translation and it is better to just ignore them. Cf. L. Lörincz, 'Vers und Prosa im mongolischen Gesser', *Acta Orientalia Hung*. 24: 1971, 51–77.

59 Corresponding to chs 8, 9, and 10a in Heissig's classification of the eight 'new' chapters. See W. Heissig, tr., *Helden-, Höllenfahrts- und Schelmengeschichten der Mongolen*, Zurich: Manesse, 1962, 81–167, 306–307. Cf. W. Heissig, *Geser-Studien*, 8 and 14–15.

60 C.R. Bawden, *Mongolian Traditional Literature. An Anthology*, London-New York-Bahrain: Kegan Paul, 2003, 223–40.

61 L. Lőrincz, tr., *Geszer Kán, a tíz világtáj ura* (*Geser Kan, The Lord of the Ten Regions of the World*), Budapest: Europa Könyvkiadó, 1982. The poetical passages are in verse form in italics. The book contains numerous illustrations.

made by teams of Mongolian and Chinese scholars from Inner Mongolia. The former is not only a full version of the GK in Chinese prose, but has also a number of poetical passages rendered in italicised verse form. Although quite free, it is the best Chinese version available at present.[62] The latter, completed in 1987 but actually published in 1989, is the Chinese translation of the popular abridged Mongolian version by Ǐirumtu published in Huhehot in 1985.[63] Although it is, therefore, an incomplete translation of the GK, it has the advantage to offer to the Chinese readership a nicely produced and readable shorter version of *both* volumes of the 1956 Peking-Kökeqota edition.[64]

A new and no doubt excellent Chinese translation by Professor Dulaan of the Department of Oriental Languages and Literature, Peking University, is being prepared and, hopefully, will be published before long.[65]

The elegant Japanese translation by H. Wakamatsu of Kyoto Prefectural University is likewise done on the revised edition of Ǐirumtu.[66]

As for Korean, the volume with the prose and verse translation of W.-S. Yu of Seoul National University has the great advantage of containing a photo-reproduction of the GK in much reduced but still legible size.[67] All the alliterative passages of the GK are meticulously rendered in Korean verse form with alliteration.

62 *Beijing ban 'Ge-si-er zhuan'* (The Peking Blockprint of the 'Biography of Geser'), a joint translation of the Research Institute of the Academy of Social Sciences and the 'Geser' Working Bureau of the IMAR, Huhhot, 1985.

63 Ǐirumtu, ed. & rev., *Geser-ün üliger* (*The Story of Geser*), Huhhot: Öbör Mongɣol-un arad-un keblel-ün qoriya, 1985. The editor has considerably revised the 1956 Peking-Kökeqota edition retaining, however, most of the contents of the latter in abbreviated and simplified form to make it more readable and comprehensible to the contemporary general reader. This revised edition consists of 12 chapters (seven of the GK plus five new ones).

64 Na-ri-su (Narasu), tr., *Ge-si-er de gushih* (*The Story of Geser*), Huhhot: Nei Menggu renmin chubanshe chuban faxing, 1989. For the editorial committee see the page opposite the Foreword (page 1). This translation is entirely in prose.

65 Personal communication of B. Ulaan of 20 October 2015.

66 Wakamatsu Hiroshi, tr., *Geseru-Han monogatari. Mongoru eiyū jojishi* (*The Story of Geser Khan. A Mongolian Epic Poem*), *Tōyō Bunko* 566, Tokyo: Heibonsha, 1993.

67 Yu Wŏn-su, tr., *Geser Khan. Mongol taesŏsasi* (*Geser Khan. The Great Mongol Epic*), Seoul: Sagyejŏl ch'ulp'ansa, 2007.

The Present Translation

The version that we offer to the public is not a literal translation of the GK nor a literary one. Our primary aim has been to make a difficult and rather unusual text in Mongolian not only accessible to the general public, but also as readable and enjoyable as the subject permits. Smooth and reliable — this is what we have tried to achieve. Hence there are no passages in brackets except for those that, from the context, are obviously parenthetical in the original. On those occasions where an explanation in the translation itself is necessary for the understanding of the text this is added after a dash. Therefore, all that is inserted between the dash and the full stop, or between dashes, is not in the original. Whereas long and unnecessary repetitions are not regarded as boring or superfluous in Mongolian they are in English.[68] For this reason in a small number of cases they have been left out in translation and substituted with a short expression to the same effect.

Footnotes have been added to explain background matters and supply essential information on a variety of topics related to the subject, and on technical terms. We have kept them to a minimum and have not regarded it necessary to give bibliographical references.

In the translation and the footnotes, we have used a simplified system of transcription, that is, romanisation, of Mongolian, different from that used in the present introduction, which is the standard one used by Mongolists. Thus in the former *č* is rendered as *ch*, γ (a voiced deep velar stop) as *g*,[69] *ǰ* as *j*, *q* as *kh*, and *š* as *sh*. The word *qaγan* 'king, chief' is transcribed 'khan' throughout. Long (double) vowels in Mongolian are not marked as such.

Many of the personal names in the story are, of course, of Tibetan origin, and the original name can, in most cases, often be reconstructed from the corrupt Mongolian form.[70] However, in the present translation they are usually given as they appear in the GK, minor misspellings being tacitly corrected. Since consistency is not the forte of the Mongolian

68 In Mongolian, especially in an epic narrative, such repetitions are actually necessary and required when reciting and declaiming in public as bards do.

69 If the *g* occurs in a word or name containing the vowels *a*, *o* or *u*, it should be pronounced like the *g* in the German *wagen*, not as the *g* in English *get*.

70 See for example, C. Damdinsuren, 'Explanation of some personal names'. See above, n. 43.

version, there are occasional passages with different forms of the same name. In such cases we have given an explanation in the notes or have added an extra element or a variant form in round brackets.[71]

The various sections of the first chapter — the one we have translated so far — are not numbered in the original text, which is continuous except for the break between chapters. They are, therefore, arbitrary and used only for convenience.[72]

Only some significant passages in poetry, whether short or long, have been rendered as such following the example of the 1985 Chinese translation and Lőrincz's Hungarian version. We feel that most of the other alliterative passages in Mongolian do not lend themselves to versification in English.

If the reader is interested in furthering their knowledge of the Tibetan and Mongolian saga of Gesar/Geser, we recommend the works mentioned in the earlier section of this introduction by R.A. Stein, W. Heissig, C. Damdinsuren, N. Poppe, L. Lőrincz, V. Veit, and the other authors who have contributed to the rich and informative *Acts of the Bonn Symposia on Mongolian Epic* published in O. Harrassowitz's *Asiatische Forschungen* series.[73]

We are most grateful to Professor Sechenmöngke of CASS for graciously presenting us with a full set of the invaluable *Geser-ün bürin bičig*, and to Professor Yu Wŏn-su of Seoul National University for sending us a digital copy of the GK as well as his own translation of it. Since Professor Yu's digital copy is from a photocopy of the original blockprint in the possession of the National Library of Mongolia (NLM), Ulan Bator, we wish to thank also the NLM for making it available. Our sincere thanks to Dr P. Rykin of St Petersburg for providing an excellent photocopy of U. Sėcėnmunx (Sechenmöngke)'s *Issledovanie*;[74] Dr B. Ulaan of Peking for bibliographical and other useful data; Dr J.R. Krueger of Bloomington, Indiana, for supplying a photocopy of I. Zeitlin's *Gessar Khan*; Professor A. Sarközi of Budapest for sending

71 Usually this applies to proper names; however, changes occur in the recollection or repetition of the account of an earlier event. See e.g. the final section of ch. 1.

72 In most translations of the GK the narrative is continuous. Kozin, followed by the 1985 Chinese translation and Damdinsuren's edition of the text (1986), divides ch. 1 into 22 sections. We have reduced the sections to 18.

73 The Internet can also supply further references on the subject of Tibetan epic, Gesar, etc.

74 See above, n. 45.

us a copy of L. Lőrincz's *Geszer Kán*; Professor G. Barmé formerly of Canberra for the loan of relevant publications; Professor A.D. Cendina of Moscow for sending additional material on Geser; and Professor B. Batjav of Ulan Bator for helpful suggestions.

For any errors or omissions, the translators are solely responsible.[75]

75 Igor de Rachewiltz is responsible for the Introduction and the draft translation of Chapter 1. Li Narangoa, a native Khorchin Mongol, has revised the draft and dealt with many textual problems.

Chapter One

Section I

A long time ago, before Buddha Shakyamuni attained nirvana,[1] the god Khormusda[2] went to pay homage to him. After Khormusda had paid his respects, Buddha gave him the following command:

> Five hundred years hence the world will go through a period of turmoil: the strong will overcome the weak and wild animals will seize and devour each other. Go home now, but after five hundred years have elapsed send down one of your three sons, for he shall become the ruler of the world. Enjoy your heavenly bliss for five hundred years, but then dispatch your son promptly according to my instructions.

Khormusda gave his pledge and returned. However, he forgot Buddha's command and did nothing for 700 years. Then, all of a sudden, at the western corner of the great city of Sudarasun,[3] the wall collapsed for the length of 10,000 miles. The 33 gods[4] with Khormusda at their head all took arms and called out, 'Who has demolished this city of ours? We have no foe nor mortal enemies; could the legions of the *asuri*-devils[5] have caused such ruin?' But when they reached that corner of the city wall, they saw that it had collapsed of its own accord.

Khormusda and the 33 gods held a consultation and together tried to work out the cause of the event. Then Khormusda remembered: 'Before Buddha Shakyamuni attained nirvana,' he said, 'I went to pay homage to him, and, having done so, he instructed me to send down one of my

1 That is, before the historical Buddha (Prince Siddharta of the Gautama branch of the Shakya clan) died, traditionally in or around 487 BC. 'To attain (enter into, etc.) nirvana' with reference to the Buddha or other saintly and exalted persons are euphemisms for 'to die'.

2 Khormusda, from Persian Hormuzd, corresponds to the Hindu god Indra, a god of the atmosphere and its phenomena, and lord of the gods of the sky. He is regarded as the protecting spirit of the earth. The capital of his heaven on Mt Sumeru is the great city of Sudarshana where Indra rules over his 32 lesser gods or *devas*, all residing on 32 peaks of Mt Sumeru. He is usually represented holding a thunderbolt or *vajra*.

3 Sudarasun = Sudarshana; see n. 2.

4 That is, 32 plus Khormusda, see n. 2.

5 *Asuri* (Sanskrit = *asura*) are a class of powerful demons with whom the gods, especially Indra (Khormusda), are at constant war. They are believed to reside in the ocean north of Mt Sumeru.

three sons in 500 years because there would be turmoil in the world, with the strong overcoming the weak and wild animals seizing and devouring each other. I forgot his command and let not only 500 but 700 years pass without doing anything about it.'

A great feast was then held by Khormusda and the 33 gods, after which Khormusda dispatched a messenger to his three sons.

The messenger addressed Amin Sakigchi,[6] the eldest of the brothers: 'Sir,' he said, 'your father, Khormusda, orders you to go into the world and become its ruler.'

To which Amin Sakigchi replied, 'I am indeed Khormusda's son. Even so, were I to go, I shan't be able to sit on a throne as ruler of the world. And if the son of the god Khormusda goes into the world and is incapable to govern it, the good name and authority of my beloved lord and father will surely be ruined. It is not that I do not relish to go; I am just unable to rule.'

Having been told this, the messenger went to his younger brother Üile Bütügegchi[7] and said, 'Sir, your father Khormusda's command is for you to go and become ruler of the world'.

Üile Bütügegchi replied, 'Am I not the son of the god Khormusda? Are not the living beings that inhabit the world the people of the yellow earth? If I were to go among them I would not be suitable to rule over them. For someone senior to me to become their ruler why not go to Amin Sakigchi? Or, perhaps, to the younger brother Tegüs Chogtu.[8] What concern is it of mine anyway?'

So the messenger went to see Tegüs Chogtu, to whom he conveyed the previous command. Tegüs Chogtu said, 'If you want an elder brother, Amin Sakigchi should go. If you want a middle brother, Üile Bütügegchi should go. How does this concern me? If I had to go I would certainly go, but if I turn out to be incapable of ruling, would it not affect the good name and authority of my beloved royal parents?'

6 'Guardian of life'.
7 'Accomplisher of deeds'.
8 'Most illustrious one'.

The messenger then reported in full their words to Khormusda and the 33 gods. Khormusda summoned his three sons and said to them, 'When I told you that the world would go through an age of turmoil and enjoined you to go to its aid, it was not my own command. It was on Buddha's express order that I did so. I thought that you were my sons, instead you have now become my father and I your son. Therefore, you three take over my rule and, as befitting, carry out all my duties whatever they are!'

After Khormusda had spoken thus, the three sons removed their hats, knelt and bowed, saying, 'Alas! Why does your lord and father utter such words?'

Amin Sakigchi respectfully addressed Khormusda: 'One cannot refuse one's royal father's command to go even if one is unfit to occupy the throne. But if Amin Sakigchi, the son of the god Khormusda, comes into the world and is incapable to rule over it, won't the people of the earth deride you saying that I was wrongly sent to them as the son of a god, utterly disregarding my younger brother Üile Bütügegchi who, as is known, can do anything?! On the occasion of the great feast in Esrua's realm,[9] when the 17 gods held games and took part in the archery contest, no one could outdo Üile Bütügegchi, who turned out to be the undisputed champion. Also, when the 33 gods met for the archery and wrestling contest, again no one was able to surpass him. And at the games held in the nether region of the dragon kings,[10] he, likewise, was unequalled in each of the contests. In every field, Üile Bütügegchi excelled. It would be futile for us, the other sons of a god, to be sent into the world — he is the only one qualified to go.'

The 33 gods said, 'Everything Amin Sakigchi has just said is the pure truth. Whatever Üile Bütügegchi does, he is better than us. In any contest, be it archery or wrestling, he defeats us all. Amin Sakigchi's words are entirely true.' So they spoke, and the younger brother Tegüs Chogtu fully agreed with them, confirming their statements.

Then Khormusda spoke: 'Well, Üile Bütügegchi, this is what they all say. Now what do you have to say to that?'

9 Esrua is a transcription of Ishvara 'Lord', the epithet of the supreme god Brahma.
10 Sanskrit Nagaraja, a title for the tutelary deities of lakes, seas, and other places.

'What am I to say', he replied, 'but that I will go into the world as my lord and father orders me to do. Khormusda, my venerable father, give me your pitch-black armour that sparkles like shimmering dew. Give me your white helmet, on the front of which sit the sun and the moon side by side. Give me 30 of your white arrows with notches of turquoise, your formidable black bow, and your neat, sharply pointed three-fathom-long black sword. Give me your golden horse-catching pole called Prestigious, your large, 93-pound steel battleaxe as well as your small, 63 pound steel axe, and your 90-pronged iron catching-pole. Grant me all this when I am born into the world.'

'Very well,' said his father Khormusda, 'I shall give them to you!'

Üile Bütügegchi went on: 'Allow also three of the 33 gods to be born into the world from the same mother as mine, to be my three supernaturally incarnate sisters.[11] Let one of the gods take my shape and become my elder brother, and from among those other gods in your suite who are the best, send down 30 to be my brave guards. It is not that I make such demands out of greed as you send me into the world. It is because once there, should I, Khormusda's own son, fail to assume its rule and be overcome by men, your good name would surely suffer. But, if by curbing the ferocious and ruthless ones on earth I bring peace and happiness to the living, this will make good my request.'

Khormusda and the 33 gods all said, 'How can we not agree? How can we be sparing with regard to what you say about your mission? We shall give you everything!'

'Fine', said Üile Bütügegchi, 'but my two brothers Amin Sakigchi and Tegüs Chogtu did refuse to go. So, after I have come into the world and been of help to mankind, it will be my turn to sit on the throne of my lord and father!'

Again they replied, 'Granted'.

Üile Bütügegchi continued, 'Dear father of mine, give me also your mighty broadsword made out of loadstone'.

'Granted.'

11 The supernatural births of the future Geser Khan's three sisters by Gegshe Amurchila is described in detail in Section II.

'And after I am born into the world, please give me a fine horse that no living being can control but me.'

'Very well, I shall!' said Khormusda.

Section II

After these events, as the world experienced a period of turmoil, a large gathering took place by the Küseleng Cairn. Besides humans, there were birds and creatures speaking 300 different languages, with the White Goddess Ariya Alamkari acting as interpreter. Also present were Moa Güshi, Dangbo, and the King of the Mountains Ua Günjid. These three together, acting as soothsayers, prepared the omens for divination.

Ariya Alamkari said, 'You three soothsayers cast the omens and find out whether or not a king will be born who can put an end to the unrest in the world'.

After casting the omens, Moa Güshi spoke: 'Boa Dongjong Garbo will be born with a topaz-like body, snow-white teeth, the head of a *garuda* bird,[12] golden-yellow tousled hair with the hair-tips spread out like willow catkins. When she is born, she will become the ruler of the highest gods.'

'Well', said Ariya Alamkari, 'let's cast the omens once again!'

The soothsayer Dangbo then took the omens and spoke thus: 'Ariya Avalori Odkari will be born spreading a white radiance and with a reddish-brown face. The upper part of her body will have human form, the lower part will be that of a snake, like the body of the kings of the dragons. She will become the ruler of the dragon kings.'

'Well now', said Ariya Alamkari, 'you, the King of the Mountains Ua Günjid, cast your omens!'

12 *Garuda* (Mong. *garudi*), a mythical bird and king of the feathered race, enemy of the serpent race and, like the phoenix, associated with fire.

'Irjamsad (= Jamso) Dari Odam[13] will be born, snow-white in colour and with her radiance spreading in all directions. She will become the ruler of all the *dakini* deities.'[14] So spoke Ua Günjid.

'Once more one of you condescend to cast the omens!' said Ariya Alamkari. This was done and the response was the following:

'Geser Serbo Dongrub will be born. In the upper part of his body he will be endowed with the supernatural power of the Buddhas of the Ten Quarters,[15] in the middle part with that of the Four Great Gods,[16] and in the lower part with that of the Four Great Dragon Kings.[17] He will become the ruler of the inhabited world,[18] Lord of the Ten Quarters, the merciful and wise Geser Khan.'[19]

The White Goddess Ariya Alamkari asked further, 'Will they all be born from the same father and mother or from different parents?' The omens were taken again.

The response was: 'The father will be the King of the Mountains Ua Günjid', they said, 'and the mother will be Kü Bayan's daughter Gegshe Amurchila.[20] As they will give each other support, they will be born of the same parents.'

'So', continued Ariya Alamkari, 'the father being this one and the mother that one, from whom will they descend?'

---

13 Many of the names in this section are Tibetan or 'mongolised' Tibetan names. In some manuscripts, the Tibetan form of the name is given in preference to the mongolised one, for example, Jamso instead of Irjamsad. The 1716 version has the latter.

14 *Dakini* or *dagini* (Sanskrit *dakini*) is a heavenly fairy 'who walks on air'.

15 The 10 regions or realms situated in the 10 directions of space — the eight points of the compass (E; SE; S; SW; W; NW; N; NE; Zenith; Nadir). There is a Buddha for each quarter.

16 That is, the four Buddhas, guardians of the four quarters/directions (Sanskrit = Maharaja).

17 See n. 10. Here, 'four' refers also to the quarters or directions of the earth.

18 Mongolian Jambutib (from Sanskrit Jambudvipa, lit. 'Rose-apple continent') designating specifically India, but also broadly the whole Asian continent, hence the known world.

19 This is one of the full designations of Geser Khan with his various epithets. See the Introduction of this volume, also for the name Geser Serbo Dongrub of Tibetan origin.

20 Gegshe Amurchila, the name of the future earthly mother of Geser, is also a hybrid Tibetan-Mongolian name: Gog-za Amurchila. See the Introduction of this volume.

To which the soothsayers replied: 'Geser Khan is the son of Khormusda, who, in turn, acts on Buddha's orders in the knowledge that an age of turmoil will prevail in the world. However, we do not know whether he — Khormusda's son — will also appear in the world in other transformations.'[21]

At that time, there were three great tribes: the Tusa, the Dungsar, and the Lig. The leader of the Tusa was Sanglun, that of the Dungsar was Chargin, and the leader of the Lig was Chotong. Chotong possessed three excellent geldings: a roan so fast that it could overtake a swiftly hurled rock; a fox-brown one that could outrun a fox; and a fawn-coloured horse that, on a zigzag course, could overtake an antelope.

When the armies of these three tribes were about to move against Kü Bayan, Chotong, jealous of the other two leaders, rode ahead on one of his fine horses and informed Kü Bayan that the armies of the Tusa, Dungsar, and Lig were fast approaching. The daughter of Kü Bayan, Gegshe Amurchila, fled to safety but, as she ran, she slipped and fell on the ice, and was seized by Chotong. However, in the fall, the young woman tore a thigh muscle and was limping. Chotong, seeing this, devised the following plan, saying, 'If I take with me this lame woman, I will lose my reputation, but if I give her to someone else, such as my elder brother Sanglun, I shall be able to take her back later'. And so, Sanglun was pressed to take her as wife, whereupon the muscle in her leg recovered and she became exceedingly beautiful and attractive.

Seeing this, Chotong could no longer restrain himself and said, 'Such an exceptionally handsome wife is hard for us to get and you *had* to father a fine son by her, but no fine son has yet been born. The present unrest in the world is, therefore, due to the two of you — husband and wife.' He consequently decided to drive away Sanglun and Gegshe Amurchila and to seize Sanglun's former wife, his house, and the cattle. He gave the couple a speckled camel with a speckled young one, a piebald mare and foal, a speckled cow and calf, a motley ewe and lamb, a spotted bitch with her pup, and a large, crooked and shabby tent, and banished them to a place at the confluence of three rivers.

21 That is, it is not known whether Khomusda's son will assume other incarnations on earth; in other words, whether he will be reborn in the world as other 'beings' (lit. 'transformations' or 'incarnations': in Mongolian *khubilgan*) besides Geser Khan.

In exile, old Sanglun busied himself trapping field rats[22] around his few head of cattle. On one day he caught about 10, on another seven or eight. Gegshe Amurchila gathered fuel. Once when she had gone out for fuel, she saw ahead of her fluttering a hawk with the chest of a bird and the hind part that of a human being. Gegshe Amurchila called out to him, 'How is it that your chest is like that of a bird but your backside is that of a human being? What sort of portent is this?' The hawk replied, 'My bird-like chest is such because I do not yet know my noble mother's relatives. The human back is due to the fact that in coming here I destroyed my original body. I came into the world from the gods above and I am now searching for a worthy woman to be reborn from her. If I am born as a human, it will be from such a woman. If I do not find her, I shall remain as I am!' With these words, the hawk flew away.

On the night of the eighth day of that month, when Gegshe Amurchila was on her way home after gathering fuel, she encountered a huge man, at whose sight she fainted in fright. At the crack of dawn, after lying on the ground for a while, she recovered her senses and headed home. A light snow had fallen, but she retraced her route. In doing so, she noticed that someone else had been striding the path, leaving footprints one-and-a-half fathoms apart.

'What sort of far-stepping man has been here?' she asked herself, and followed his footprints. The trail led to a cave in an enormous rock. Gegshe Amurchila peered into the cave and saw a man sitting on a golden chair. He held a banner, variegated like a tiger,[23] and wore a dress and boots of similar kind.

The man sitting on this golden chair, which was supported by a toadstool, was wiping the hoar frost off his beard and saying, 'Tonight I have really exerted myself to the utmost'. At this, Gegshe Amurchila was frightened and hurriedly returned home.

22 Mongolian *ogotona* — a vole, of which many species are present in Mongolia.

23 An ornamental staff and, at the same time, a symbol of authority.

The beings speaking 300 languages dispersed and the White Goddess Ariya Alamkhari ascended to heaven. The soothsayers, Moa Güshi and Dangbo, went up the Küseleng Cairn. They had all been waiting for the fulfilment of the prophecy. 'It has been fulfilled!' they cried and they too went on their way.[24]

Section III

After Gegshe Amurchila's return home, her belly began to grow, so that she could no longer stand up or sit down. In the morning of the 15th day of that month, when the old man took his pole lasso and was about to leave to muster his cattle, Gegshe Amurchila called out, 'Why do you leave now? In my belly there is a continuous sound as if several people were conversing with each other. I am scared to death of being left alone. Stay with me today!'

Old Sanglun said, 'If I stay with you, who will hunt the field rats and look after our few head of cattle? If I do not catch field rats how are we going to make a living?' And without further ado, he went off, set his traps and caught 70 field rats. The old man carried them back full of joy, saying to himself, 'Today I caught many more than usual; surely my house will be blessed!' At home, he unloaded the field rats and went off again.

Then, in the afternoon, from the wife's belly a child's voice broke out in song: 'I, Boa Dongjong Garbo, will be born with a topaz-like body, snow-white teeth, the head of a *garuda*-bird and golden-yellow tousled hair with the hair-tips spread out like willow catkins. I shall become the ruler of the gods on high.'

Thereupon another voice sang: 'I, Ariya Avalori, will be born with a white radiance and with a reddish-brown face. The upper part of my body will have human form, the lower part will be that of a snake, like the body of the kings of the dragons. After my birth, I shall become the ruler of the dragon kings of the nether regions.'

24 The prophecy in question is the forthcoming births of the gods' incarnations, especially that of Geser, which are the subject of the next section that begins with Gegshe Amurchila's discovery that she is pregnant.

Then one more voice sang: 'I, Irjamsad (= Jamtso) Dari Odam Odkari, will be born, snow-white in colour and with my radiance spreading in all directions. After my birth, I shall become the ruler of the *dakinis* of the Ten Quarters.'

Then another voice sang: 'I, Geser Serbo Dongrub, will be born with the upper part of my body endowed with the supernatural power of the Buddhas of the Ten Quarters, the middle part with that of the Four Great Gods, and the lower part with that of the Four Great Dragon Kings. After my birth, I shall become the ruler of the inhabited world, the merciful and wise Geser Khan, Lord of the Ten Quarters.[25]

'Alas, woe is me!' cried the mother, 'What kind of Buddha would ever be born to me when not even an ordinary mortal has any need of me and I was driven away to a desolate place where three rivers merge?[26] A brood of devils incarnate — that's what will be born to me! No one is providing food and sustenance to your poor father, old Sanglun, let alone preparing the cradles for the four of you. No one is looking after me, let alone nursing and taking care of you in this tiny tent the size of a bird's nest. However, I shall now try to find a place here to accommodate you.' So saying, with a nine-fathom-long iron stake used for digging out silverweeds, she dug four separate pits, each four fathoms long.

While she was still busy with it, Boa Dongjong Garbo crying, 'Mother, make room for me!' fell out from the top of her head, in figure and appearance beautiful beyond description. She crawled down, slipping out of her mother's grasp and, as the mother tried to get hold of her, an elephant made of precious topaz, complete with saddle and bridle, was sent by the gods on high. It pulled up amidst the sounds of cymbals and drums and the burning of incense. With this accompaniment, the child was raised on to the topaz elephant and taken to heaven.

'My dear one was truly a Buddha', said the mother, weeping.

She was still crying when a voice called out: 'Elder sister,[27] make room for me!'

25 See nn. 15, 19.

26 Sanglun and Gegshe Amurchila had been banished by Chotong to a place at the confluence of three rivers (*belcher*). I have added the word 'desolate' because it is implied. As we shall see, the merging of these three rivers had created a great lake.

27 Referring to the child that had just preceded her, not to the mother.

The mother lifted her right arm and pressed the top of her head, and, in doing so, another child fell from her right armpit, crawled off, and again escaped her mother's grasp. In the meantime, from the depths of the ocean, the dragon king sent an elephant, made, as the one before, of precious topaz and likewise saddled and bridled. Amidst the sounds of cymbals and drums and the burning of incense, the dragon king took the child and carried her off to the depths of the ocean.

Then one more voice called out: 'Elder sister, make room for me!'

The mother, squeezing both her armpits, pressed the top of her head with her hands, and out of her navel fell another child — one far more beautiful and charming than the other two. However, the mother was again unable to get hold of her. While she was reaching for her, the *dakinis* of the Ten Quarters arrived with a sky-blue elephant duly saddled and bridled, and amidst the burning of incense and the beating of cymbals and drums, they took the child and left.

'Alas! Alas! My three dear ones have gone', cried their mother and wept. 'What they said about them being incarnations of the Buddhas has all come true. Whatever for have I dug those four-fathom-long pits? How unbearable! If only I had been able to recognise one of you so as to greet and embrace you, and kiss you before we separated! But alas, my dear ones have gone', she cried and wept.

As she was thus lamenting, another voice called out: 'Elder sister, which way shall I come?'

'Be born the natural way, my darling', said the mother loudly. And so the boy was born the normal way. At birth, he was squinting with his right eye while with his left eye he looked straight ahead. His right hand was waving around while his left one was clenched into a fist. His right leg was lifted upwards while his left leg was extended forward, and his 45 snow-white teeth were tightly clenched. 'Alas! Alas!' cried the mother, 'what shall I do? The three who were born before to me were all incarnations of the Buddhas and this is why I could not hold onto them. But this strange child is the incarnation of the devil and, no doubt, is bound to stay with me! Now my darling, with what shall I cut your umbilical cord?' Whereupon she took a large knife kept inside her pillow and attempted to severe his umbilical cord. But the knife could not even cut into it.

'My dear mother', said the child, 'that big knife of yours cannot sever my umbilical cord. Go and collect a sharp, black stone, which is on a bank inside the great lake in front of our tent. Cut the umbilical cord, and, while you do that, recite the following prayer: "My dear one, may you be a living being stronger than this stone!" Then, tie up my navel with a plain blade of grass, saying: "My dear one, may your beloved people become more numerous than the grass in the field!".'

The mother then wrapped the child in her skirt and proceeded in haste to the great lake. She took the black stone from the bank inside the lake and cut his umbilical cord while uttering the appropriate words. She then tied up his navel with a plain blade of grass saying the prayer as told above.

When Geser was born, a fine, cold rain was falling, and, as the mother was about to cut his umbilical cord, her little finger became frostbitten. 'This naughty wicked child,' she cried, 'just as I was cutting his umbilical cord I got my little finger frostbitten!'

'Do not swear at me, my dear one, and do not weep', said the child. 'Dip your little finger in the waters of the great lake and see what happens.' The mother did what the child told her and her little finger became as healthy as before. Afterwards, she took the child home.

Once there, she asked him: 'Dear one, where shall I put your cradle? Shall I put it in this hollow?' As she picked him up, however, the child slipped from her grasp and fell to the ground. The mother lifted him up again but once more he slipped down.

As he struggled with her, he declaimed as follows:

> Dear mother! My right eye is looking sideways
> So that I can stare angrily at demons and devils.
> My left eye is looking ahead of me
> So that I can see straight at what destiny has in store.
> My right hand is swinging
> To strike at all my adversaries.
> My left hand is clenched into a fist
> To hold everybody in my power.
> My right leg is lifted upwards
> To promote the Buddhist doctrine.
> My left leg is extended forward
> To bring down and trample on heretical and false doctrines.
> The 45 snow-white, tightly clenched teeth I was born with
> Are meant to utterly destroy the might of the fiercest demons.

So he spoke, and 'Alas! Alas!' his mother cried, 'When children are born, their fourth fingers usually cover their nostrils and their eyes are usually closed. What sort of spiteful and sharp-tongued creature is this child of mine, so quarrelsome and contentious from the moment he was born?' She was, thus, wrangling with him when Sanglun returned home. Now he could hear a woman's voice, now something like the roar of a tiger.

Old Sanglun was driving home his cattle, carrying 10 field rats on his back and dragging his nine-pronged iron catching-pole with one hand. 'What is going on here?' he asked.

Gegshe Amurchila said, 'You miserable, good-for-nothing old grumbler! You luckless wretch! Did I not ask you to stay with me today? A short while ago my three children left me to go wherever they had to. They were all born as incarnations of the Buddhas: the one who had to rise to heaven rose to heaven, the one who had to descend to the realm of the dragon kings did so, and the one who had to go up to the region of the *dakinis* went up to them. Who knows which one said "heaven above", "the dragon kings below", and "the *dakinis* of the Ten Regions"; as soon as they were brought forth, they happily went their way. And right now, you miserable wretch, no sooner have I given birth to another child — a devil incarnate — who, judging by the way he acts, already intends to devour me!'

'Ah, you!' cried the old man, 'How do you know that he is, in fact, a devil's incarnation? Your knowledge may be only a baseless suspicion. Are we Buddhas? And how can we kill our own child? Let us instead try to bring him up! Today I killed 80 field rats. These few miserable heads of cattle I have are all pregnant. They are increasingly dragging their bellies along the ground. At the beginning, near our home there were no field rats to be found. Today, within the distance of a whistling-arrow's shot, around the house no snow has fallen. I have never witnessed such a thing in my whole life, as it was within this very distance that I caught the field rats and I doubt it was the catching-net or my catching-pole that did it.[28]

'If it is as you say,' replied the mother, 'we cannot kill the child. And if we are going to raise him, let us try to raise him well!'

28 That is, 'that made me bring this bounty home'.

Section IV

At that time, a devil in the guise of a black raven used to peck the eyes of infants, thus blinding them or even killing them. Having heard of Geser's birth, this devil approached him to peck out his eyes, but Geser recognised him through his magic powers. He closed one eye while looking sideways with the other fixed on his nine-pronged iron catching-pole. Just as the black raven devil came to peck out his eyes, he pulled the rope of the catching-pole, caught the black raven devil and killed him outright.

Also at that time, another devil would appear with teeth like those of a goat, and the snout of a dog. He used to transform himself into the Güngü Echige Ergeslong (= Gelong) lama.[29] While laying his hand on the head of one-year-old children[30] as if to bless them, he would bite off the tip of their tongue, thus making them dumb for good. Geser knew this and was aware that the devil was also coming for him, so he clenched his forty-five snow-white teeth and lay in waiting. The devil came in the guise of the lama, placed his hand on Geser's head in blessing and tried to insert his finger between the teeth. Then he tried to insert a horn spike[31] but was unable to prise the teeth open.

'Did your child have a tongue at birth or was he born like this, unable to open his jaw?' the lama asked Geser's parents.

'We don't know — he cries all right', they replied. Then the lama-devil put his own tongue in the child's mouth for him to suck it. The child sucked a little.

'Good, he sucks the tongue!' said the devil, and gave it more tongue to suck. Geser, pretending to be sucking it, bit the devil's tongue off right at the very root,[32] thus killing him.

---

29 *Gelong* is the Tibetan designation of a Buddhist mendicant monk (Sanskrit *bhiksu*) who depends on alms for a living. In later usage it designated a Buddhist cleric (lama) who has received the highest ordination. *Echige,* 'Father', is just a term of respect.

30 'Two-year-old' in the text. Mongols, like the Chinese and other Asian people, are reckoned to be one-year-old at birth, hence two years = one Western year.

31 That is, a fid or spike like a thick needle made from the horn of a gazelle and used for untying knots.

32 Lit. 'right through the windpipe'.

Then the accursed field rats suddenly grew in size and became like oxen, turning over the surface of the earth[33] and doing much harm to the Mongolian people.[34] When Geser heard about it he changed into an old cowherd, took his axe, and ran after the field rats. As they were growing into oxen, spoiling the landscape in the process, the old man struck the oxen between the horns with his axe, dispatching them all. There and then he killed the Three Terrible Ones.[35]

After that, a ewe gave birth to a snow-white lamb. Then a mare gave birth to a bay foal of great wisdom, a cow gave birth to a turquoise iron calf, and a bitch gave birth to a copper female pup with an iron snout. To all these, Geser made an incense offering and prayed to his heavenly grandmother Absa Kürje as follows: 'My dear grandmother, take care of all these creatures of mine and rear them well. When I ask for their return please give them back to me!' Then he gave them all to Absa Kürje to take them upwards. Grandmother agreed and took them with her.

Old Sanglun gave the name Joro[36] to the son born to his long-suffering wife. Joro looked after their few heads of cattle. As he was tending them, he pulled out three times seven stalks of reeds and did the same with the feather-grasses *deresü* and *kilagana*, and with the twigs of the caragana.[37] With the *deresü* feather-grass he lashed his old and weak mare saying, 'I shall keep on lashing you with this feather-grass of mine — with three lots of seven stalks each time — until you bear me a herd of horses as yellowish white as this *deresü* feather-grass!' Then he lashed his poor old cow with the reed stalks, saying, 'Bear me such fine cows in a colour like the seeds of these reeds and with tails like their stalks!' With the *kilagana* feather-grass he lashed his sheep, saying, 'Bear me many lambs as fine as this *kilagana*!' And with the caragana twigs he lashed his mangy camel. All the animals without exception brought forth their young: the single mare produced a herd of horses as white as the *deresü* feather-grass —

33 Lit. 'epidermis' (= surface, crust). In the ancient Mongolian conception of the world, Mother Earth was covered with a 'brown epidermis'. 'Brown oxen': the text has 'fawn-coloured oxen (or cows)'. The gigantic field rats 'turned over' the surface of the earth because, as field rats, they continued to make burrows and live underground.

34 Please note here the first reference in the text to the Mongolian people.

35 This seems to be an interpolation. The *dogshid*, lit. 'Terrible (or Wild) Ones', were wrathful and awesome-looking deities of the Lamaist pantheon acting as judges, protectors of religion and executioners, but they are usually eight in number.

36 This name (Joru, 'bastard', in Tibetan; see the Introduction of this volume, n. 29) is variously transcribed as Joro, Joru, Juru, Jürü, and Dzur in Mongolian depending on the dialect. We have adopted the form Joro, already popularised in the West by I.J. Schmidt.

37 All common plants and shrubs (the caragana) of the Mongolian grassland.

but surely there is no need to go through them in detail. Every month they would duly bear offspring, in compliance with Geser's command, so that the cattle increased beyond reckoning.

Old Sanglun's happiness knew no bounds. 'My prayers have done it!' he cried. 'As they say, "One is but the beginning of a thousand".'

To which Gegshe Amurchila replied with tongue in cheek, 'You are absolutely right, of course, about that, what else? And I certainly know a lot about your prayers and how exceedingly lucky you are. But who is now going to tend all this cattle of ours?'

Then Sanglun proceeded to the main camp of his people, went up to Chotong and said to him, 'From that beautiful and fine woman of yours, whom you drove away because of ill-feeling, an ordinary boy was born. If he turns out to be worthless, I can keep him with me, but if he is capable should he not become a khan? And, even if he is worthless, he is entitled to the throne by right of succession.[38] Now, you return to me my wife, my children, my house, and cattle!'

All the people said, 'He is right! How could it be otherwise?' So, his family and all his possessions were given back to him. Sanglun took them and returned home.

Thereupon Sanglun said, 'You three, Jasa, Rongsa, and Joro, together will properly tend my cattle'. The three children[39] set out to do that, but Joro, by means of his magic powers, made the distant mountains seem near and the near ones seem far away, and, in this way, he herded the cattle. He said to his father, 'What is the purpose of your rejoicing, because, thanks to your prayers, the cattle has increased? Why don't you now build a white palatial tent for yourself?'[40]

The old man replied, 'Do we have the strength and skill to get hold of the timber for it? Let's go and try!' They went to the forest, and together began to fell trees. The old man at first felled plane trees and chopped up several of them. Joro, by magical means, erected tent walls with proper wall sections, and made rafters with suitable poles.

38 Lit. 'having the rank (*or* dignity) of succession' — Joro being the son of Sanglun who was Chotong's elder brother. But the fact that Joro's mother was Gegshe Amurchila must have also played a role.

39 Jasa and Rongsa are Sanglun's children from his earlier wife he has just brought home.

40 That is, an imposing white felt tent suitable for a chief — white being the sign of wealth, nobility, and rank.

Old Sanglun saw a beautiful plane tree and went to cut it, but, at that moment, Joro employed his magic and turned it into a thorny tree. Thus, the old man's hands became lacerated and he could not cut the tree down. 'Here again goes that awful child!' cried Sanglun. 'I was just felling a beautiful plane tree when it turned into a thorny tree. I cut my hands and, once more, I return home flustered and empty-handed!'

Then Joro came, bringing the timber for the white palatial tent. 'My dear father,' he said, 'you came, leaving behind the wood you cut and piled up. I have come now, bringing the tent made with the wood you had cut.'

'Certainly,' said the father, 'I cut the tree, but lost the spot where I felled it and left it there, and now this wretched thief has stolen it and is keeping it!'

'Your words are true, my dear father', said Joro. 'My timber, which I stole from yours, is enough for several tents. You felled the tree. I lacked the strength for it, and with the wood you cut I made the tent frames.' And he had the tents covered with felt.

Section V

Sanglun harboured a special affection for Rongsa's mother. After the three boys set out to tend the cattle herd, the mother would cook their meal, which she then laid out and served on one table for Jasa Shikir[41] and Rongsa. For Joro, however, it was poured into a dirty dog bowl.

Once, Joro took three handfuls of white and three handfuls of black pebbles. He placed the white pebbles on a rock, and all the cattle grazed on their own.[42] When it was time to return from the pastures, he would put the black pebbles into his pocket and set out for home, whereupon all the cattle followed him of their own accord.

The following morning, the three of them went again to tend the cattle. Later, as they sat chatting, Joro said to his two elder brothers: 'While we are made to look after such a large herd of cattle we are always poor and hungry. Let's slaughter a calf and eat it!'

41 Jasa, here and later, is given the epithet of Shikir (or Shiker) 'Sugar'.
42 That is, without being herded or getting lost.

'Slaughter a calf and eat it?' Rongsa said. 'Our parents will be very angry with us. I say no!'

Jasa Shikir sat and kept silent.

'I shall take responsibility for the scolding and the rest. You go, Jasa, and catch a calf!' said Joro.

Jasa caught one. Joro killed it and removed its skin, shaping it like a leather sack. After they had eaten the meat, Joro placed the bones inside the sack, grabbed it by the tail and tossed it around three times. By then, the sack had turned into a live calf, which ran after all the other calves. The three brothers herded the cattle together and made their way home.

When they entered the tent, Jasa and Rongsa remained standing, while Joro sat down at his place on the left and began eating his meal. 'Why is Joro eating and you two are not?' asked Rongsa's mother.

Rongsa replied, 'Brother Joro slaughtered one of our calves and gave us the meat. We have had plenty and we do not want any more food.'

Old Sanglun asked, 'What, Joro, is this true about you?'

To which Joro said, 'I won't say it is a lie.' The old man then seized his whip and jumped up to strike Joro, who, throwing himself against the whip, grabbed it and started to fight with him.

While they were struggling, Gegshe Amurchila came running. 'What is the matter with you, old man?' she asked.

'This fiendish son of yours took a calf, killed it and ate it — such a contemptible thing to do!' said Sanglun, unable to contain his fury.

'You miserable and foolish old grumbler!' she railed at him. 'Have your calves become numberless now? You should take stock of them first! How have they become so many for you to own, old fool? Even if it is true that he has eaten one, how can you thrash my son because of a single calf? You seem to believe that the cattle has increased only thanks to your good care.'

So she spoke, and the old man ran out to check his calves. They were all accounted for, so he ran back home and vented his anger against Rongsa, saying, 'What a liar you are! If in future you lie to me again I shall thrash you within an inch of your life.'

The following morning, the three boys went to take the cattle out. Joro again slaughtered one, and Rongsa secretly hid its tail in his bosom. As before, they ate the meat and put the bones into the sack. When Joro tossed it around three times, it turned into a short-tailed calf, which ran off along the trail after the other calves. The three of them then gathered the cattle and made their way home.

There Rongsa said, 'Let us eat the tail of the calf our brother Joro slaughtered for us!' He produced the blood-spattered tail from his bosom and buried it in the ashes of the hearth to roast.

The old man said, 'Rongsa, what are you doing with that?'

'Our brother Joro slaughtered a calf and served it to us', replied Rongsa. 'I am just cooking its tail to eat it.' 'Now, dear Joro,' cried the old man, 'how could you do such an awful thing again?' He seized the whip to give him a thrashing, but Joro threw himself against the whip and snatched it away from him. 'If there is one who is old and feeble-minded it is this one! Why does he rush at me and want to beat me? Why does he attack me?' he called out. Joro's mother came running. 'What's the matter with you, miserable old boor, what's wrong now?' said she.

'Rongsa said that Joro slaughtered another calf and Rongsa himself is now roasting its bloody tail. Isn't that the truth?' replied the old man.

To which Joro's mother said, 'How can you on the strength of your son's baseless words start a beating? Count your calves first and find out!' The old man counted the calves: they were all there, only the tail of one calf was still bleeding.

'He has cut off the tail!' cried the old man. He rushed back home and gave Rongsa a good thrashing, saying, 'Why do you falsely accuse this poor boy? As they say, "When the illegitimate child comes home only the watchdog feasts him."'[43]

43 The meaning of this unusual saying is, we think, that an illegitimate offspring is not welcome in his original household — only the yurt's dog is happy to see him. The reference is to Joro being so disliked by his half-brother Rongsa, who clearly regards him as Sanglun's bastard son.

But Joro retorted, 'It is destined that, instead of being accused falsely by him, I shall actually be accused with good reason. It is destined that tomorrow I shall kill many of your cattle but will not partake of them!'

The three boys went out with the cattle. Joro killed nine wethers from the herd of sheep and, by magical means, assembled several large cauldrons, dazzling Rongsa with his majestic aura. He cooked the meat, and when he had removed it from the cauldrons, he burnt incense and addressed the following prayer to all his guardian spirits:

My reverend father, God Khormusda on High!
And also the 17 gods of Esrua's realm
And the 33 gods who are at your side;
Absa Kürje, my dear grandmother, and
Arya Alamkari — my interpreter — the White Goddess;
My life's guardian spirits
Who speak 300 different tongues;
My soothsayers Moa Güshi and Dangbo, and
My incarnate father on this golden earth,
Mountain King Ua Günjid;
My victorious three sisters;
My worthy protecting Buddhas of the Ten Quarters;
My four great dragon kings of the nether regions!
When you all said to me 'Go!'
I came and was born in the world.
Now, after my birth, to you all
I show you the worthless person I am,
I bow to you and offer you this pure sacrifice.

All the guardian spirits said, 'Our Snotty has been born on earth![44] Our nose can smell the delicious scent of his offering: this is the sign to let us know that he is already down there.'

Having thus prayed to all his protectors, Joro placed the food before Jasa and Rongsa on a big table for them to partake. Jasa sat and ate his fill with great zest, but Rongsa, who was still overwhelmed by Joro's majestic aura, sat and ate nothing. Joro then assembled the guardian spirits, who, in the guise of a great number of people, ate everything up. At this point, Rongsa hurried home while Jasa and Joro together went to tend the cattle.

44 Lit. 'golden (= yellow) earth'. 'Snotty' (*nisukhai*) is a term of endearment for children, but in the case of Joro/Geser it will become his common nickname in his early youth.

At home, Rongsa spoke to his parents, saying, 'Your son Joro has cut open and slaughtered nine wethers, and having collected several cauldrons has boiled all their meat. When the meat was cooked he took it out and began shouting nonsense like "Heaven on High!", "Kings of the dragons below!" and "Oh! Oh! Buddhas!" He spoke a lot of nonsense, which I did not understand. Then he brought the meat to Jasa and me, but, because I felt so upset on account of the sheep, I did not eat any. I don't know where all our cattle has gone. While we were eating, a lot of aimless people and passers-by came along. He foolishly rushed to meet them crying "Bu! Bu!" and took their horses. That lot then had a feast and gobbled up all the meat.'

So spoke Rongsa to the old man, who, crying 'How evil! How wicked!' grabbed his whip and ran out to look for the cattle. He went up a hill and looked around, shielding his eyes with his hand. The herd was all close to Joro, but the old man could not see the animals because Joro, with his magic powers, had dimmed his sight. The old man rushed back home. 'All of a sudden I cannot see a thing! Alas, what a shame. Just you wait, Joro!' he cried, and went on threatening him. No sooner had the old man uttered his threats that Joro, singing a song noisily, drove the cattle home.

'So, you are the real singing boy. I recognise you!' the old man said, brandishing his whip and moving to thrash Joro. But, as he was about to hit him, Joro snatched the whip and flung it away.

The old man wrestled with Joro, who, pretending to fall down, cried 'Oh dear!' and threw him over his head.

The old man shouted 'Oh! Ah!' in a rough voice; Joro did the same, shouting 'Ouch! Ouch!'

Gegshe Amurchila came running in and asked, 'What is going on, old man, what is it?' 'I thought you had given birth to a child', said he, 'but what you were saying is true: he is the incarnation of a devil, cutting open, killing and eating nine wethers. When I tried to punish him, he threw me over his malicious head a few times. I wonder whether he has crippled me. My body hurts terribly.'

'If he has crippled you', she replied, 'that's that! When Rongsa earlier repeated that Joro had killed a calf, was that true? Now you are saying that he has slaughtered nine wethers. That he has thrown you over his head seems to be true, but you should check the number of wethers even so.'

The old man went and counted the wethers. They were all there. On his return he cried, full of sorrow, 'Ah, Rongsa! Whatever for have you done that?'

Gegshe Amurchila said, 'And you, dear Joro, what are you going to do about it? As the saying goes, "The man who built the house stays behind while the one who cut off the branches goes in front."[45] Rongsa wants to kill you. Now he came to report you. If, because of Rongsa's words, the old man wishes to give you a thrashing with his whip, Rongsa will oblige by killing you with his knife. I see all sorts of troubles for you ahead.'

Joro then reprimanded Rongsa: 'Before you came back, I bred the herd of cattle singlehandedly, and singlehandedly, without any quarrels, I looked after it. Had I killed some everyday, how could the herd have multiplied so? What is the reason for your vicious hatred toward me? Why do you wish to start a fight with me with your endless lies?' Thus he reproached him. Rongsa did not utter a sound, but Jasa chuckled.

The old man said, 'Well, then, Rongsa, is this not the pure truth? If in future you but open your mouth I shall give you a very sound beating!'

The following morning, the old man thought to himself, 'You, three sons of mine, are unable to get along peacefully. I shall now herd the cattle.' Taking Jasa with him, he drove the cattle to pasture, and tended the animals without any trouble. In the evening, they drove the cattle back. The following day, the old man again took Rongsa along when he went out. As the two of them were looking after the cattle, three sheep were seized and devoured by wolves. When they returned home in the evening, the old man said, 'While I was herding the cattle and this good-for-nothing was looking after the sheep, he let three sheep be taken and be devoured by wolves'.

45 A saying possibly illustrating a reversal of role. The man who builds a house should come before the one who cuts the timber for it. Gegshe Amurchila criticises her son for not taking the initiative by letting his brother Rongsa go ahead with his murderous plans. We are not sure, however, that this is the correct interpretation.

Joro sat down and said, 'Had it been me, you would have certainly beaten me up. Fortunately, however, the fact that you did not take me along with you has turned out to be fine for me.'

The next morning, the old man drove his cattle out to graze, taking Joro with him. Joro made the distant mountain seem closer. While moving along the edge of the sheep herd, a wolf ran past him. 'Father dear, do you know what that wolf is doing running about?' he asked.

The old man replied, 'What do I know? He must be on the lookout for a sheep.'

'Well then, father, you shoot one arrow at that wolf. If you hit him, slaughter a wether and do not share the meat with me — eat all of it yourself. If you miss, I will take a shot, and if I hit the wolf I shall slaughter a wether and eat up the meat myself without giving any to you,' said Joro. The old man agreed and shot an arrow at the wolf but missed. 'Is it my turn now, father?' asked Joro.

The old man said, 'That's right'. Joro shot and the arrow hit the wolf. He gave its skin to him, saying, 'Dear father, you are an old man. Make yourself a warm waistband with it.'

Then, Joro, by magical means, killed nine sheep and assembled a number of cauldrons. While he was grabbing the sheep, the old man cried, 'Alas! Joro!' but could not produce a sound. 'Oh! Get away! Stop it!' he shouted, but couldn't even stand up, and, unable to raise his voice, he now sat quietly and looked on.

Joro took the mutton from the pots and, as before, called and gathered his many guardian spirits. To the old man, they appeared as many people setting a table and dishing up food, but being still overwhelmed by Geser's majestic aura, the old man could not eat. Joro, on the other hand, being magically transformed into many people, ate his way through all the meat. They both got up from the table. The old man rushed home while Joro saw to the cattle.

On arriving home, the old man complained to his wife: 'It is so, my dear, what shall I do then? What Rongsa told us is the absolute truth. Joro has slaughtered nine wethers and devoured their meat all on his own. It is true what you said of him, Gegshe Amurchila, that he is a devil: either one of the malignant spirits or a *manggus*.[46] Having disposed of our herd, he will come to take us and eat us up!'

After the old man had vented his grievances, Joro came along, driving the cattle home. 'Dear Joro, there is no more doubt about you, either you are a tiger or a wolf, isn't that so?' said the old man, striking him repeatedly with his whip.

Joro seized the whip and asked the old man why he was doing that, to which he replied, 'Why did you destroy those sheep?'

'Let's go!' said Joro, 'You and I will not part ways here. Jasa will judge who is wrong!' And so they went, Joro leading the way. They came to Jasa and let him decide the case.

The old man spoke: 'This fool Joro and I together went with the sheep when a wolf ran alongside the flock. This stupid lad then asked me whether I knew why the wolf was running about and I said that he must have intended to eat a sheep. "If so", he said, "let us make a bet!" "I don't mind if we do, but what is the point?" said I. "You shoot at the wolf. If you hit him you kill a sheep and you do not give me even a mouthful. You eat the meat you have earned all by yourself", said he. I agreed. "If you miss and I shoot and hit the wolf, I shall eat up the sheep in precisely the same way", he declared and I said, "Fine!" We both took a shot but being an old man I missed. Joro shot and killed the wolf.' Then both Joro and the old man related in detail how they had been eating the mutton on that occasion.

Jasa said, 'When yesterday you and Rongsa together went with the cattle and allowed three sheep to be seized and devoured by wolves you did wrong. To shoot on a bet, dear father, was also an error on your part. Now, old man, keep quiet and go your way!' 'The character and behaviour of my sons is quite different from mine', said the old man and went away.

The following day, the old man again took the cattle and went out with Joro. A magpie was perched on a tree near the herd of horses and the oxen, and a fox was running to and fro near the oxen. Joro said, 'Father dear, do you know why a fox and a magpie are so close to our cattle?' The old

46 Originally (13th–14th c.) the term *manggus* designated a large snake or dragon. In time, and under the influence of Buddhism, it was applied to a cruel and monstrous creature, a sort of ogre (Sanskrit *rakshasa*). Because of its ill-defined demonic nature, we left it untranslated.

man replied that he did not know, to which Joro said, 'The magpie intends to peck at the horse's saddle sores and gradually penetrate the spinal cord; the horse will then surely die. The fox has been chewing some grass that the cows eat so that they will gradually be poisoned and die. What else? Let the two of us shoot and kill both of them. The one who does will then slaughter and eat an ox and a horse, and will give nothing to the other, not even a taste!' The old man, happy because the fox was quite near, tried to stretch his bow but Joro with his magic had disabled it.

'Ah! I give up!' said the old man. He kept on pulling at the bow with a bitter look but was unable to stretch it.

'Hurry, father!' said Joro. The old man hesitated, then shot and missed. Whereupon Joro took a single shot, killing both the magpie and the fox with it. He gave the fox to the old man. From the horse herd, he chose a fat mare, and from among the cattle a fat ox, and slaughtered them both. The old man was about to protest but could not utter a sound. Joro cooked the meat and again set up a table and offered some to the old man who, however, was unable to eat any of it. Thanks to his magic, Joro ate it all up. He then settled down and sang:

A magpie wanting to peck at the horse's sores,
A fox wanting to poison the cows,
An old man wanting to shoot them both dead:
What is more shameful
Than any of these three?

The old man got up and rushed home. He said to his wives, 'Well, now, I can no longer get along with him. After he has eaten all my cattle, he will devour me. From the way he acts, this one is not a devil, he is most certainly a *manggus*!'

Section VI

Determined to find out who was the best of his three sons, the old man caught a partridge with a net and put it into a leather sack, tying up the opening. Then he rode off with Jasa on a *khainag*.[47] The partridge in the

47 The *khainag* is a cross between a yak and a Mongol bull or cow. This hybrid is subsequently referred to as *üker*, 'horned cattle', to be understood here simply as 'cow'.

sack grew restless and the *khainag* bucked, throwing off the old man, who then lay on the ground and pretended to be dead. Jasa called out, 'Father dear, did I not ask you to teach us how to hunt, to instruct us on how to dismantle the yurt and move across the country?[48] Alas, how can we manage now without you?' Crying and wailing, he returned home. The old man, too, made his way home, riding the *khainag*.

The following day, the old man rode off, again with Rongsa sitting behind him. Like before, the *khainag* bolted and threw the old man on the ground, where he lay as if dead. Rongsa just cried and turned back. The old man mounted the *khainag* and went home too.

The morning after, he once more rode off, this time taking Joro with him. As they were going, they saw a Chinese tilling a field, at the edge of which was a magpie hopping over a wooden fence. As before, the partridge became restless, the *khainag* bucked, the old man was thrown off, and he lay on the ground as if he were dead. Joro leisurely dismounted, and, holding on to the *khainag*, started loudly wailing and crying. Then he ceased making noise and said, 'Even the mountain can vouch for my crying, and the trees on the mountain too! If this wicked Chinese had not been ploughing his land, setting up a wooden fence at the edge, surely the magpie would not have risen from it, the *khainag* would not have bucked, and my old man would not have perished!' He went straight for him, exclaiming, 'I will give that Chinese his desserts!'

Joro then repeated to the Chinese word for word what he had said earlier, adding, 'I shall now take you, a living being, to replace the dead man. Come along with me!' The Chinese, however, did not pay any attention to him, whereupon Joro proceeded to destroy his cultivated field. The Chinese, distressed by what he was doing to his land, rushed to him, crying, 'Whatever you command I shall do as you say, but do not destroy my field!'

'You will compensate me for your misdeed. Cut down and bring me wood from this mountain. I shall use it to burn the body of my father!' said Joro, and the Chinese complied. Joro then placed the wood all around his father and lit a big fire. When this was ablaze, the old man cast a look sideways at Joro, who forthwith threw a handful of soil in the father's eyes, forcing him to close them. Joro said, 'It is said, dear father,

48 The text simply says 'on how to travel'— on how to decamp, move across country with the cattle and other animals, and set up camp on new grounds as the Mongol nomads did.

that it is a bad omen for a dead man's living offspring if he died with his eyes open'. The old man became very afraid of being burned, so he curled up, bending his legs. 'It is said that the line of the surviving wife and children will not stretch long if both legs of the dead man are bent at the time of his death,' said Joro, lifting a huge log and placing it across his father's legs. Then he lifted him and carried him towards the bonfire.

As he was taking him over to throw him into the fire, the father shouted, 'Joro dear, your father is not dead, he is alive!'

At which, Joro exclaimed, 'Father dear, they say that it is a bad omen for the surviving descendants of a dead person if this person makes an apparition'.

With these words, he was just about to throw him into the fire when the old man cried, 'But my dearly beloved, I am not dead, and you are going to kill me while I am still alive?'

'Dear father of mine, it is wonderful that you are not dead', said Joro, and having put him on the *khainag* returned home with him.

When he arrived home, the old man said to his first wife, 'I went with my three sons to tend the cattle in order to test the good and bad qualities of each of them. My Jasa will become quite a brave man; my Rongsa will be one who eats on the sly — an ordinary man — but on every occasion neither will match my Joro.' And, very pleased with himself, the old man went out.

His wife, however, conceived an evil scheme: 'How is it', she thought, 'that the son born to a rejected wife[49] can be better than my two sons? I shall dispose of him immediately.' So she laid out nice food on the table for her two sons, but for Joro she prepared another dish, containing poison. In the evening, she fed the three boys: Jasa and Rongsa came, sat down at the table and ate their meal, while Joro remained standing on the left, watching. His stepmother said, 'Dear Joro, why do you stand there and watch? Take your seat at the table and eat your meal.'

Joro walked up quickly to the table, took hold of his bowl of food, sat down and said to his brothers, 'Until now, our dear, elderly parents have given us our share of the family provisions. From today, they will give

49 It will be remembered that Joro's mother, Gegshe Amurchila, had been rejected by uncle Chotong after her accident, and he gave her to his brother Sanglun.

us our share of the family livestock. You two, elder brothers of mine, are guilty of misappropriation because you did not make the customary *degeji*-offering of food to our parents.[50] What matters if I do not eat anything myself?' He therefore gave his food to his father as the offering. Unwittingly, the father took the bowl and was about to eat when Joro snatched it and gave it to the stepmother instead. She took it and, out of shame, was ready to eat from it, but Joro took it away again, and saying 'From old this big pot has served us as the family cooking pot', he poured some of the food into the pot, which immediately cracked. Then he dropped some on the brazier, which then fell to pieces. He threw some upwards into the roof-ring, which also shattered into pieces. Saying that the yellow dog was also part of the household, he poured some food over the dog's head, which split in two. He himself partook of what was left in the bowl, squeezing out the reddish poison, and offered it as sacrifice to his elder sister, who was with the kings of the dragons.[51]

Section VII

Old man Sanglun moved back to the main camp of his people and settled with his family and belongings at the camp's edge. Chotong Noyan[52] saw them while he was out hunting, and exclaimed, 'Such a splendid white yurt — whose is it and to whom do those countless cattle belong? We must go and ask who owns the yurt and the herd.' He sent a man ahead, who reported that they belonged to old Sanglun. Chotong Noyan, with all his suite, went over to Sanglun's yurt and asked who had given him so many head of cattle and the white yurt. Joro then approached him and said, 'Are you like a file that does not recognise its iron, like

50 *Degeji* is the first serving of the choicest part of something (food or drink) offered to a deity as a sacrifice or to a noble guest.

51 That is, to Ariya Avalori, whom we met earlier — Geser's sister destined to become the ruler of the dragon kings of the nether regions. The text says that Joro squeezed out 'the *ulabar* ("reddish")', which must be the name of the poison still found in the food previously doctored by the stepmother. This was almost certainly a poisonous plant, part of which was reddish in colour. In modern Mongolian the term *ulaavar* (= *ulabar*) by itself designates only *Ilex crenata* Thumb., but in combination with other words is applied to several other unrelated plants. This entire section is descriptive of the pranksome nature of young Joro, and how his magically contrived pranks are essentially motivated by his desire to redress the wrong and castigate the evil that pervades the world, beginning with his closest human relatives.

52 The bad uncle Chotong is given here and throughout this section the princely title of *noyan*, which he bore as the leader of his people, the Lig tribe. However, in the GK, the use of titles, alternative names and nicknames is inconsistent.

a dog that does not recognise its parent? Because you drove away your own elder brother, the gods above, and the kings of the dragons below, all of them together pity him and have given him a dwelling and the cattle.' 'Look at him', he added, 'such a scoundrel!'

Chotong Noyan said, 'The Seven Ogres,[53] so they say, daily catch and devour 700 men and 700 horses irrespective of their predestined fate.[54] Let's do them a favour for good luck and offer them both Joro and his mother. You two are to leave the camp today. The Seven Ogres will surely catch you and devour you. In the coming days, I will supply them with other humans!'

Joro said, 'Good!' and laughed.

But his mother exclaimed, 'My dear one, what is to be done? How can you laugh about it? When I gave birth to you, I thought you would be a reliable, good son, but instead I have given birth to a thoroughly bad one. Did Chotong not say that the Seven Ogres catch and devour 700 men and 700 horses a day? Did he not say that the two of us must go along to be seized and devoured?'

'Be quiet, mother dear. You, as a woman, cannot understand this. If we stay here, uncle Chotong will kill us. If we go, the Seven Ogres will eat us there — the motive is the same', said Joro, and loading their crooked and shabby tent on the two *khainag*, Dangkhar and Dongkhor moved to the Boljumur Valley.[55] When they reached the edge of the valley, they stopped. Joro set up the crooked tent, lit a fire for his mother, and went out hunting.

When he came back, having killed 14 field rats, Joro roasted seven and stewed the other seven. In the evening, the Seven Ogres came along, each preceded by 100 men bent in submission and followed by 100 bent horses.[56]

Joro went out to meet them. 'Ah, wise Geser Khan, Lord of the Ten Quarters, why did you come out yourself?' cried the ogres.

53 *Dologan albin.* Apparently these were a subclass of demons notorious for their rapacious hunger.

54 That is, without taking into account the law of karma that ultimately determined their destiny; in other words, regardless of whether they deserved to perish that way or not.

55 Lit. 'Valley of the Lark'.

56 The men and horses driven by the Seven Ogres were bent in fear and despair since they knew what awaited them, *viz.* becoming the ogres' next meal. From what follows, however, it appears that the latter recognised in Joro the future Geser Khan, and were themselves in awe of him.

'You had us frightened to death!' Joro replied. 'I heard a deceitful rumour to the effect that you daily catch and devour 700 men and 700 horses regardless of their predestined fate. Because of that, my uncle Chotong has sent me to you to be devoured, saying that he would supply you with other humans in the future.' 'O merciful and wise Geser Khan, Lord of the Ten Quarters, why do you speak such words, scaring us to death?' exclaimed the ogres.

Joro said, 'Well, if you do not intend to devour me then deign to stop at my shabby yurt and partake of my tea and soup before riding on.' The Seven Ogres dismounted and Joro offered them the 14 field rats, but the ogres, without consuming even one, mounted their horses to depart. Joro said, 'I will teach you one magic feat if you give me your seven horses'.

The ogres consulted each other and said, 'Alas! If we give you the seven horses, on what are we going to ride?'

'Ride on these seven white magic sticks of mine', said Joro, 'and while going at full speed, keep saying "Cut across the mountain!", "Cross the plain!", "Trample the rock to bits!", "Knock down and uproot the bush!", "Cross the ocean!" These sticks of mine will be much better mounts than your seven horses.'

The seven Ogres agreed with joy, got off their horses and departed in haste, riding the sticks. They rode on, and all along the way they kept saying 'Cut across the mountain!' They progressed speedily, following Geser's instructions exactly. They then said among themselves, 'We have been riding so much just as if we were horse racing. Geser says that in the ocean it is even better going, and that as soon as we enter it, all will be fine.' And so they plunged in, but no sooner were the seven white sticks were in the middle of the ocean that they changed into seven fishes, and the Seven Ogres sank to the bottom, perishing. The seven white wooden sticks returned to their owner. So, Geser, through his magic powers, killed the Seven Ogres and took their horses.

Section VIII

At that time, a band of 300 Sartagchin[57] menials and robbers with their noisy children came with their wagons to hunt near Joro's yurt. Joro knew all about them because of his superhuman powers, and magically produced a polecat endowed with a golden breast and snow-white claws. He then went over to meet those people and let the polecat play games and show off its beauty. Seeing the polecat, the 300 strangers stopped hunting and watched the performance with real pleasure. At sunset, Joro took his polecat and returned home.

The strangers retired for the night, but the same evening one of their men came over and said to Joro, 'Hey, man! You are a sort of relative of ours. Give us your polecat on loan. We'll let it play a while and then we shall return it to you!'[58]

Joro replied, 'If you lose my polecat will you give me your 300 geldings in exchange?'

'We'll give them!' said the man.

'Are you the person making this request on behalf of your headman,' asked Joro, 'or are you speaking independently, for yourself? Better go and ask him first!'

The man went and asked the headman, who said, 'Certainly, we'll give them. Bring the polecat!'

The man returned, confirming that should the polecat be lost they would give up their geldings, whereupon Joro handed it over with the warning 'Mind you don't lose my polecat!'

The polecat, however, had Joro as his master and that very same night returned to him. The following morning, Joro rose early and went across to demand the return of the polecat. The people there looked for it, even under the cauldrons, but there was no polecat to be seen. They told Joro, 'Your polecat must have dug a hole in the ground and made his escape'.

57 A general term for the Muslim inhabitants of Central and Western Asia who, since early times, travelled and engaged in trade. Here, they are portrayed like gypsies (in derogatory Western usage).
58 Clearly, these strangers had no intention to return the unusual performing polecat to Joro.

Joro replied, 'Do polecats came down from heaven above? You knew that they come out of the ground but decided to take a gamble and avoid returning it to me, isn't that so? Now give me my 300 geldings as we agreed!'

'Of bold men,' said the headman, 'you are the boldest. Why don't you take our 300 geldings yourself?' With these words, they all went off. Joro followed them on foot. As they were passing through a gorge between two very high mountains, he hastily climbed to the top of a nearby peak, dislodged a huge rock and threw it with force against the peak on the other side. On being struck, it shifted position, thus also shaking the peak on this side, so that both mountains trembled, and the falling rocks hit the people and their horses below from all sides. They then fled nearby on Joro's side, but there too they were knocked to the ground as before.

They cried out, 'O merciful Holy One, if you kill us, as you are doing, in such a cruel manner, what is your command? We shall do whatever you order!'

'There is no command from me,' said Joro, 'just give me back my polecat!'

'We do not have your polecat, but will obey any other order of yours', they replied.

To which Joro said, 'If so, then shave off your beards and hair, embrace the faith and take the vows!' All of them, men and women, came and had themselves shorn. Having thus converted them to the Buddhist faith, Joro-Geser took their 300 geldings and returned home.

Outside Joro's crooked and shabby tent, the horses of the Seven Ogres and the 300 horses of that band of Sartagchin were grazing. Joro spent the summer with that large herd of geldings out in the open fields.

Section IX

In the meantime, at home, his elder brother Jasa Shikir was lamenting him, saying, 'Chotong Noyan got angry with my Snotty Joro and sent the Seven Ogres to seize and devour him. Did they catch him and eat him? If so, I shall fight them to death. If he is alive, I shall pay my younger brother a visit!' He saddled his winged grey horse, wore his scaly armour, covered his noble head with the helmet called Prestigious,[59] placed 30 white arrows in his quiver, seized his black bow, put on his hard sharp sword of the finest steel, and proceeded to the Boljumur Valley.

At the edge of the valley, he saw a herd of geldings. 'The Seven Ogres have surely taken and devoured my Snotty Joro!' exclaimed Jasa Shikir, and thrusting forth his sharp steel sword, he struck the thighs of his winged grey horse and charged ahead. Then he saw, standing in the middle of that herd, Joro's crooked and shabby tent. Tying up his horse in a hidden spot, he pulled out his fine sword and, without making a sound, quickly crept up to the tent and peeped inside. What he saw was Snotty Joro sitting in the yurt, undressed because he was perspiring. Jasa sheathed his sword and rushed inside.

'My dear Jasa!' cried Joro, getting up and running towards him, the two of them embracing and shedding tears. As they were hugging and crying, the golden earth shook and trembled.

'Had I died, my Jasa, you would have come and perished with me at the hand of the Seven Ogres. And had I stayed alive, you would still have come to visit me. This, my dear one, is the true mark of your heroism! Quiet now!' said Joro, and, making an incense offering, appeased the rumbling earth. Then he continued, 'Am I not, dear one, your Snotty Joro? Am I not also the Lord of the Ten Quarters, the merciful and wise Geser Khan? Indeed I am both, but do not tell this to anyone, my dear, because until I am 15 years old, I as Joro will utterly suppress the ruthless and the violent, and only after that shall I reveal myself as Geser and take you all as my companions.' Jasa Shikir laughed for joy.

59 In the epic tradition (both East and West), as well as historically, it is not only horses that have names or epithets, but also weapons such as swords, armour, etc. Names of famous swords are recorded in Chinese texts of the third century BC. In Section I, 'Prestigious' is the name of Khormusda's horse-catching pole.

'You, Jasa,' said Joro, 'take these 300 geldings and give them as a present from me to my poor father. The seven horses you take yourself. And, my dear brother, be reassured that death does not touch me!' Jasa Shikir then turned back, mustering the herd of geldings.

Chotong Noyan met him on the way and asked Jasa from whom he had got those many geldings.

He replied, 'I have killed the Seven Ogres who had caught and devoured Joro, and I have seized their geldings'. 'Good riddance to a bad character! I am glad you came back safe and sound.' So said Chotong and went off.

Jasa gave the 300 geldings to his father, whereupon the old man cried with joy. 'Well,' he said, 'this child of mine is surely different to me now!'[60]

At that time, there was a *manggus*-ogre called Ir Tonggorog, who had settled on top of the Kürme Pagoda. It reached towards the sky, so that to the people who lived south of the pagoda he blocked the morning sun, to those who lived west of it he blocked the midday sun, and to those who lived north of it he blocked the evening sun. He was also able to see a person at a distance of a full day's journey away and would take and devour anyone who was half a day distant from him.

Joro knew of him. He transformed himself into a poor and dirty marmot trapper. As such, he went to the pagoda, where he started digging a hole near its base. While he was lying down and excavating, the *manggus* called out and asked him, 'Who are you?'

Joro replied, 'Oh gracious one, may I be permitted to disturb you a little? I am but a miserable marmot trapper trying to kill a marmot. One has just run into this burrow and I am lying here in order to dig it out.' The *manggus* resumed his position without saying anything, so Joro continued to excavate the foundations of the pagoda, digging from the nearest side to the farthest. Then he gave it a strong push, and the pagoda fell, breaking into four or five large fragments. The *manggus* fell from the top of the pagoda, crashed down and died. Having thus disposed of him, Joro packed his crooked and shabby tent and returned home with his mother.

60 That is, from what he used to be in the past. Most translators read, 'This child of mine is surely not different to (= he is just like) me!'

When Joro reached the main camp, Chotong Noyan saw him. 'Why, it's Joro!' he exclaimed, 'Jasa had told me that you had been caught and devoured by the Seven Ogres and that he had killed the ogres and seized their geldings'.

Joro said, 'And now you wonder whether the two of us, Jasa and I, have been up to something — that we have ganged up on you?'

'Maybe yes, maybe no, but the way you are acting, I would say yes!' said Chotung.

'His father is with you: why did Jasa tell lies about me?' said Joro, and left.

Section X

Once again, Chotong Noyan, filled with hatred, came back and declared, 'Today our camp will move to the Boljumur Gorge. Joro and his mother will go and settle at the Engkerekü Ridge.'[61]

'Very well!' said Joro, and chuckled.

'How can you laugh so, my darling?' cried the mother tearfully, 'I was happy thinking that I had given birth to you as a reliable and good son; instead, it turned out that I produced a hopelessly deficient one. Are you not aware, dear son, that in the so-called Engkerekü Ridge no rain falls in summer, but there are heavy snowfalls in winter that turn into regular snowstorms? That there is no *argal*,[62] no firewood, and no wildlife? Such is the bare and withered region this place is said to be. Is he not sending us there so that both of us, dear one, may perish? Rather, let us settle alongside Chotong's people and make a living weaving wool!'

Thus she spoke, and Joro replied, 'Be quiet, my dear, as a woman you do not understand. They say, "A goat seeks its mate. After butting each other they separate. A woman seeks a companion. After quarrelling they part."[63] Let us proceed, my dear one!' Joro took his mother and together they left for the new location. After Joro had reached Engkerekü Ridge and they had established themselves there, the place turned into

61 Lit. 'Favourite (or Loving) Ridge' — obviously an ironic or fanciful designation.
62 Dry dung of animals traditionally used as fuel, 'buffalo chips'.
63 A proverb illustrating *sensu lato*, the inevitability of conflict and separation in life.

a beautiful and prosperous encampment. Through a passage, Joro had water pouring in from the great lake, and all around the yurt he planted trees that produced every kind of fruit. All manner of game came in great numbers to this place, which Joro named Chakirmag Khogoltu.[64]

One day, when Joro was hunting on the Engkerekü Ridge, a caravan of 500 merchants of the Erdeni Khan of Taski, who were returning from a visit to the Tayibung (Taiping) Emperor of China,[65] passed by, bringing with them valuable goods. They had everything except, perhaps, a pair of ordinary human eyes; in fact, they were fully equipped. Joro, with his magic powers, transformed himself into two parts: one consisting of a band of 20 men, the other of a swarm of stinging bees and wasps that immediately surrounded and attacked the caravan.

These merchants, seeing no way in which they could proceed, and with death staring them in the face, cried out, 'O Gracious and Holy One, we did not recognise you! These treasures of ours: if you wish to obtain them take them to your heart's content, but if you wish us to become your friends and followers, we shall become your friends!'

'Very well, let us get going!' said Joro. 'You will build me a splendid residence like the temple of the Qomsin bodhisattva (= Avalokiteshvara).[66] Build it of gold, silver, and iron, mixed with stone.' The 500 merchants first built a stone bridge over the great lake, then they erected huge stone pillars. The rafters of the building were made of iron, the window frames of lead, and within each frame they inserted bright, precious stones so that the light was allowed to penetrate inside the house. The roof was made with gold-plated silver lining, the ridges being set with sparkling jewels. Then, inside the building, they erected a statue of the Qomsin bodhisattva, and in the four corners of the mansion, they placed bright

64 Possibly meaning something like 'place having calling (= enticing) food'.

65 Both unidentified personages, although some scholars claim that Taski = Tajik. Erdeni ('Precious') and Tayibung (Chinese Taiping 'Pacific') are just epithets. Read 'from the ruler of Taski to the emperor of China'.

66 That is, the Chinese Guan(shi)yin or Goddess of Mercy, being the female representation of the bodhisattva Avalokiteshvara, a major deity of the Buddhist Mahayanic pantheon, which enjoyed immense popularity in Tibet, Mongolia, and China, embodying in its various manifestations the power of universal compassion.

and luminous gems. In front of the bodhisattva's image, they fixed a chindamani precious stone.[67] If a stone was pulled out of the arch of the bridge, ambrosia flowed out from it, pouring into the building.

The 500 merchants then addressed Joro as follows: 'Having planned to carry out all kinds of things, we have now built something that cannot be bent by wind and cannot be destroyed by rain. You need not search for light nor fragrance, and there is no lack of holy water. Oh wise khan, is everything according to your heart's desire?'

'Oh poor people, you did well!' replied Joro, 'I will now let you return home. Are you going back across our Tibet or by another route? Go across Tibet. When you pass by the yurt of Chotong, he will ask you whether during your journey you touched Engkerekü Ridge. You will say that you passed through it on the way. He will then ask you, "It's where our Snotty Joro went: is that wretch dead or alive?" This is what you will say to him: "Snotty Joro built a temple there for the bodhisattva Qomsin, made with stones, iron, silver, gold, precious glass, and lead, all of them combined. Then, Joro himself died and that building now stands there without an owner."'

So Joro spoke and, having dismissed the merchants, built a tall palisade of sharply pointed trees around the house, with only a gate for transit, and for this opening he provided a 30-fathom-long iron chain. He also prepared two three-fathom-long stakes. One stake he made into a catching-pole with the iron chain, fixing it in the ground at the gate, but in such a way as to allow a man on horseback to pass through. Then he collected some thick sticks and kept them nearby.

The merchants passed by the yurt belonging to Chotong, who went to meet them and started questioning them. The merchants repeated Joro's words as if they were their own. Chotong Noyan said, 'Good!' He then promptly mounted his black horse, attached the quiver to his belt, and made his way to the Engkererü Ridge.

Joro, who knew this through his magic powers, lay on the ground close to the chain, feigning death. When Chotong Noyan arrived, his black horse shied, frightened by the opening in the fence. Chotong whipped him on the thighs and hit him across the head, spurring him

67 Chindamani (Sanskrit Chintamani) is the legendary jewel or pearl that fulfils all one's wishes — a most powerful talisman. In the popular religion of Tibet and Mongolia, it was associated with the cult of Qomsin bodhisattva.

so that the horse got inside the fence, but was caught by the iron chain. Joro jumped up and quickly pulled out one of the stakes, winding the chain several times around Chotong and the horse. After having thoroughly bound them, he beat both of them swiftly with the sticks, whereupon he took the other stake and, after tightening the horse even harder with the chain, he loosened it and let him go. The black horse darted off out of control. 'What happened to Chotong Noyan? Has he gone raving mad?' shouted the people, pursuing him but unable to overtake him. 'Let's lunge forward and grab him!' they cried, but the horse kept changing direction. For seven days and nights, Chotong Noyan escaped capture. Eventually, the people of Tibet organised a battue: they encircled Chotong with three rows of carts, and driving him into the circle of the hunt managed to catch him. After having freed him from the iron chain, they dismounted him from the horse. Chotong Noyan stood up but could barely walk.

'Master Chotong, what happened to you?' asked everyone.

'A large group of merchants passed by my yurt and I asked them about Joro, whether he was alive or dead,' said Chotong, 'but they lied and told me he was dead. Why? Had I ever harmed them in any way, such as killing their parents? So I proceeded to Joro's place. He grabbed me, beat me almost to death, then threw me out.'

Jasa Shikir then reprimanded him, saying, 'You asked whether you killed the merchants' parents, but I now ask you whether Joro killed *your* mother and father, seeing as you banished him to a place of death such as the Engkerekü Ridge. If only my brother had beaten you to death!' So thundered Jasa, after which all the people dispersed.[68]

68 The narrative in this chapter is very terse in the original and we had to employ a freer style in English, including additional words, in order to make it intelligible.

Section XI

Joro was out hunting when he met Arulga Goa,[69] the daughter of Ma Bayan, who, having slaughtered a sheep, was making a plantain loaf with its meat,[70] which she then put into a leather bag that she carried on her back. Joro asked her whose daughter she was and why she had come this way. 'I am Arulga Goa, daughter of Ma Bayan', she replied. 'My father sent me to ask you for permission to establish his camping ground here.'

'You stay here now', said Joro, and took the dish she had just made to his mother. When he returned, he found that the young woman had fallen asleep. So he went to her father's herd and took a foal that had been born prematurely to a mare. He went back with it and wrapped it in the skirt of the young woman. Then he shouted, 'Get up! Get up!' The young woman awoke and sat up. 'What a sinful and shameless girl you are', said Joro, 'coming to me like that! Did you have an illicit relationship with your father so that you bore a child with the head of a horse? Or was it with your elder brother, so that your son was born with a horse's mane? Or with your younger brother, so that he should have a horse's tail? Or was it perhaps with an ordinary Chinese serf so that your child was born with four legs? Get up, you lewd wench!'

'Alas, what is he saying to me this one?' the young woman said, jumping up. The foal fell from her lap. 'Oh, woe is me. What a shame! What a disgrace!' she cried, 'What shall I do? Darling Joro, don't tell anyone about what has happened to me. Take me as your wife!'

'Are you sincere?' asked Joro.

'I am!' she said.

'If you are', said Joro, pricking his little finger, 'lick the blood of this finger of mine.' She did so.

69 Arulga (or Arlan) the Fair, daughter of Ma the Rich. There is no mention of them in the Tibetan Geser epos. Ma is a common Chinese, usually Muslim, surname. Arulga reappears in later chapters as Aralga.

70 That is, she mixed the chopped lamb with flour and leaves of plantain to make the meat loaf.

Then Joro took the foal's tail and tied it around her neck saying, 'This I give you as my marriage pledge to you. As for your father, only he with his group of tents must use this camping ground; no other stranger[71] will be allowed to approach it!' Thus he spoke, and the young woman returned home.

Section XII

While Joro was still hunting, Chotong Noyan went to the wedding of Ma Bayan's daughter, Machina Kimusun Goa,[72] to his eldest son, Altan. She was Chorisdong Lama's younger sister — and he was accompanying her.

When Chorisdong Lama arrived, Joro went to meet him. He grabbed the halter of his horse and addressed him: 'You are the great all-merciful Lama and I am a poor and needy man. Please, O Lama, grant me some of your bounty!'

'I am travelling in the steppe and right now I have nothing on me to offer you', said the lama. 'Tomorrow, however, Chotong Noyan is giving a great feast. Come and I shall give you of my bounty.'

'If you really want to give me something', said Joro, 'you could deprive yourself of the horse you are riding and of the coat you are wearing.'

'Just look at the insolent behaviour of this scoundrel!' exclaimed the lama, hitting Joro on the head with his whip. Joro then pulled the lama down and the two of them started fighting. Uncle Chargin came, shouting, 'Dear Joro, good Joro, let that man go, stop fighting! If I side with my *khuda*,[73] Chorisdong Lama, you, my nephew, will be angry with me. If I side with you, my *khuda* will be angry with me. Tomorrow there will be a great banquet. If you don't have anything with you, get a three-year-old goat from someone and bring it along with you.' Joro then said to

71 *Khoshun kümün*, lit. 'a *khoshun* person'. *Khoshun* is a technical term used during the Manchu Qing dynasty (1644–1911) for an administrative unit (the so-called 'banner'), regional authority or province. A '*khoshun* person' designates here someone from another region or area, hence 'an outsider, a stranger'.

72 Later referred to as Kimusun Goa ('the Fair').

73 *Khuda* is a general kinship term for a relative through marriage on the bridegroom's side; in-laws.

the lama, 'I release you because of uncle Chargin's words, but be sure that either in this world before the multitude of men, or in the nether world before the King of Hell[74] I shall disgrace you and bring shame on you!' With these words, Joro let go of the lama.

The following day, Joro asked some people for a goat. He killed it, prepared the meat, put it into a leather bag on his back, and went to fetch his mother. At the feast, from the outset, Chotong Noyan sat on a raised seat as did Chorisdong Lama, on his left, with the female guests sitting below them. The banquet began. No seat having been allocated to Joro, he took his place at the furthest end of the men's side. Since Joro's mother had not been given a seat either, she sat on the bare ground. Joro then got up, rushed out and collected some horse dung that he placed on the ground, on top of which he inserted a stalk of feather grass.[75] He split the tip of the stalk into three sections and, bending them, made a seat on which he sat.

The guests at the banquet were eating the abundance, but no one gave Joro any of the meat. When Chotong Noyan grabbed the foreleg of a sheep, Joro said to him:

'Uncle! Here is a mountain of meat
And an ocean of liquor,
But only the lucky eye can see them:
They never go down the unlucky gullet.
Give me that sheep's foreleg
That you have just grabbed!'
'I could give you the shoulder blade',
Replied Chotong, 'were it not essential
For my wealth. And the tibia too,
Were it not the lucky sign of my children.
As for the sheep's radius, to give it away
Would be the evil of all evils!
For you the bare earth, the cough,
The tears and snot of weeping men.
You take the meat of the cattle perished
On the right bank of the river.
You take the meat of the cattle perished
On the left bank of the river.

74 Erlig Khagan in Mongolian, Yama in Sanskrit — the god of death, judge of the dead, and lord of the Underworld.
75 *Deresü*, the very common tall feather, or broom-grass (*Lasiagrostis splendens*) of north China and Mongolia.

You take the meat of the dead cattle,
The ones that perished north of the river:
You take all that!
You take as wife the rejected bride,
The one who is fat and full of spots,
You take as bride a former devil!
There! This is all I am giving you!'

Joro then jumped up. 'Now,' he shouted, 'all of you listen. How ridiculous! Uncle Chotong has given me some of his gifts. He has given me bare earth: from now on, any man who digs out the root of the seal-worth and the silver weed,[76] as well as all the people who cultivate the land, must first ask my permission. If they don't, they will surely bring disgrace upon themselves, and mightily so! Chotong has given me as a gift the tears and snot of weeping men who suffer from coughs and colds. From now on, these people will have to ask my permission to cough and weep. Whoever weeps and coughs without permission, no matter what, will incur great shame! As for the meat of the horses that died on the right side of the river, of those that died on the left side, and of the sheep that perished on the north side of the great river, all those have been gifted to me by uncle Chotong and you can eat their meat only with my permission. If you don't, you will surely be in trouble! And he also told me to take a rejected bride and former devil as brides!' Saying this, Joro sprang up and tore away the clothing from Kimusun Goa.

Thereupon, Chorisdong Lama, who possessed magic powers, let a wasp come out of his left nostril and ordered it to fly to Joro and blind him in one eye. Joro, knowing this through his own magic powers, closed one eye while looking sideways with the other. Eagerly, the wasp flew towards Joro but, frightened by him, stung his lip and then returned to the lama.

The lama asked whether it had stung Joro in the eye, whereupon the wasp answered, 'I found that one was blind and the other squinted, so I stung his lip and came back'.

'Now, go up into his left nostril, strike at his brain and kill him!' commanded the lama.

76 *Ürgüne*, or *ürgene*, and *kichigine*. The first is the *Polygonum viviparum*, the second a *Potentilla* — two common herbs, or rather weeds, of Mongolia.

As the wasp approached him, Joro closed one nostril, as if it were bleeding, and used his left nostril as a trap to entice the insect. When the wasp was about to crawl inside Joro's nose, he caught it in the nostril-trap, then seized it firmly in his hand. The lama fainted and fell from his seat, and there he lay frantically biting the ground. Every time Joro loosened his grip on the wasp a little, the lama kept getting up and bowing down to Joro. If Joro again tightened his grip, the lama fell down senseless as if dead.

Chorisdong Lama's younger sister Kimusun Goa knew that what Joro had in his grasp was her brother's soul. Holding in one hand a turquoise the size of a large vulture's head and in the other a jar of spirits, she approached Joro. When she stood before him, however, he cried, 'Alas, how sad! Look at this daughter-in-law! In our country of Tibet, a khan's[77] daughter-in-law is not supposed to meet any stranger for a period of three years; the daughter-in-law of a commoner for a period of three months. This one has no in-laws and no parents — she is an odd daughter-in-law. Is this insect here your mother or your husband or your parents?' With these words, Joro turned his back to her and went away.

A hunchback, a sly officer of the law in the service of Chorisdong Lama, then came to Joro and said, 'Dear Joro, darling Joro,

Whoever in future beholds you
And gives nothing in return,
May his eyes blast!
Whoever listens to you
And gives nothing in return,
May his ears grow deaf!
Whoever eats with you
And gives nothing in return,
May his teeth crumble!
Whoever seizes something
And gives nothing to you,
May his hands break!
There is a snow-white mountain.
On this snow-white mountain
A snow-white lamb is bleating
Of its own accord.

77 Kimusun is going to be the daughter-in-law of Chotong Noyan, called here a tribal chief or khan. Note how, in this instance and again later on, Joro refers to his country as Tibet whereas before he spoke of 'our Mongolia'!

There is a golden mountain.
On this golden mountain
A golden windmill is turning
Of its own accord.
There is an iron mountain.
On this iron mountain
A blue-green cow is frolicking
Of its own accord.
On another golden mountain
There is a beater which beats wool[78]
Of its own accord.
There is a copper mountain.
On this copper mountain
A copper-coloured dog is barking
Of its own accord.
There is yet another golden mountain.
On this golden mountain
A golden gadfly is buzzing
Of its own accord.
There is gold dust which
The ants' king has collected
In the mountain gullies.
There is a golden lasso
To catch the sun with
And a silver one to catch the moon.
A hornful of blood
From the nose of the ants;
A handful of lice tendons;
A hornful of blood
From the nose of the male blackbird;
A hornful of breast milk
From the female blackbird;
A hornful of tears
From the young of the blackbird.
And in the great lake[79]
There is a juicy topaz
As big as a roller stone.

78 That is, a long stick for beating wool to make felt.

79 It is not clear whether the 'great lake' in question is the earlier mentioned lake near the home of Joro's parents, or whether 'great lake (or sea)' here means 'the Ocean'.

Dear Joro, take all these precious things as well as Kimusun Goa, only let go of this insect!' So saying, he bowed and Joro released the wasp. The lama also made his obeisance to Joro and sat on the raised seat. Joro took Kimusun Goa and gave her as wife to his beloved brother, Jasa Shikir.

Section XIII

At that time, there came Senggeslü Khan's daughter, Rogmo Goa, who had not yet found a husband worthy of her. She had brought along with her three excellent archers, three strong wrestlers, a wise lama, and many servants. These comprised her suite. She came because it was said that in the country of Tibet there lived 30 prodigiously brave men and that one of them might be a worthy husband for her. In fact, a great number of men wished to participate in the contest and were already assembling.

Chotong Noyan was also going. When Joro politely asked him whether he could ride pillion with him, Chotong replied, 'You, wretch, are going with the intent of marrying Rogmo Goa, the incarnation of a heavenly fairy, are you not? As for myself, I am going elsewhere.' He had barely gone when uncle Chargin came along and Joro asked him to be allowed to ride sitting behind him.

Chargin said, 'Come with me!'

When Chargin and Joro arrived, the throng of suitors had already assembled, and Chotong Noyan was at their head.

Joro said, 'When uncle Chotong said that he was going elsewhere, I was very happy. Actually, he is now going to secure Rogmo Goa for himself. Good luck to him!'

Rogmo Goa rose, stepped forward, and said, 'Among the princes of this land, there are surely men with outstanding skill and talent. As I said, I shall be the wife of the one who will beat my three excellent archers and three strong wrestlers — all of them. So far, no one has defeated them. You must judge such an unusual decision on the part of a noble maiden regarding her choice of a husband in light of the following:[80]

80 This passage, ending here, is a shortened and paraphrased version of the original.

When I was born,
On the western side of my house
An animal, the unicorn,[81]
Was gambolling on the roof.
On the eastern side of the house
An antelope, the saiga,[82]
Was leaping about on the roof.
It was a cloudy day
But there was brilliant sunshine.
Then the clouds disappeared
And it began to rain.
On the main rafter of my house
A parrot began to sing.
On the next rafter a cuckoo
Began to cry "cuckoo",
And on the third rafter
The beautiful Uriangkhai bird
Began to sing.
Thus you can see that I am
Rogmo Goa, the maiden incarnation
Of the most accomplished
Of all heavenly fairies.
Now go and measure yourselves
With my excellent archers,
With my strong wrestlers!'[83]

Now, if the first of Rogmo Goa's three excellent archers shot an arrow early in the morning, it would return to earth late that morning.[84] If the second archer shot an arrow, this would return to earth in the time it takes to brew tea twice. As for the third archer, tea could be brewed only once before the return of his arrow.

81 *Seru*: originally the name of the rhinoceros this term was also used to designate the mythical unicorn, a symbol of loving kindness and good fortune from ancient times.

82 *Orolug*, apparently designating the *Saiga tartarica* or antelope of the steppes; likewise an auspicious omen.

83 The translation is tentative as some Mongolian terms and expressions are not clear. The alliterative passage enumerates the unusual events that forecast the momentous birth of the future wife of Geser. 'Of the most accomplished', lit. 'of the ninth rank (or class)'. Uriangkhai is the name of a Mongol ethnic minority now inhabiting north-western Mongolia and a small area of eastern Xingjiang.

84 Others understand 'in the time it takes to brew tea thrice'. The tea in question is 'brick tea', which takes much longer to prepare than ordinary tea.

Rogmo Goa said, 'After having shot their arrows in the morning, our archers will lie on their backs. When the arrows come down, they must move their heads to avoid them: each arrow must in fact hit the exact spot where the head was. Only then shall we regard him as an excellent archer. Furthermore, even if the archer shoots his arrow very high, but in that competition the arrow does not hit the right spot on its descent, we shall regard that as a poor shot.'

Now, the 30 reincarnated heroes competed with Rogmo Goa's three archers, but none could equal them, and none was able to defeat her wrestlers. Then Joro rose, rushed forward, and asked Rogmo's lama whether, in spite of his small stature, he could have a try at the wrestling contest.

'The 30 heroes, vastly superior to you, were unable to win the contest. You better give up, dear friend!' the lama said.

'I still want to wrestle with them!' replied Joro.

'Then fight!' said the lama. Joro prepared himself and stood in readiness.

'Where are our wrestlers?' called the lama, 'This lad wishes to wrestle with them!' The strongest of the wrestlers then rose and stepped forward. At that moment, Joro assumed his true form and changed into Geser, but his transformation remained concealed to the eyes of all those present. With one foot, he stepped on the peak of a mountain; with the other, he stepped over the fringe of the ocean. He took the wrestler and hurled him a 1,000 miles away. The second strongest wrestler he threw 2,000 miles away. The third strongest wrestler he threw 3,000 miles away. All the people around watched Joro with the utmost attention.

Then, the three excellent archers shot their arrows. By noon, these had all returned to earth. By evening, the arrow shot by Joro had not yet returned, and the sky become very dark. Everybody called out, 'The sun has set, night has fallen'.

As the crowd began scattering, Jasa Shikir cried, 'No! It is dark like this because my Snotty Joro's arrow is about to come down!' He had barely spoken these words when the arrow drew near and reached the ground. Joro turned his head to avoid it and the arrow hit the spot exactly where Joro's head had rested. (Joro's elder sisters, who were ruling the skies, had caught his arrow while in flight and had stuck all sorts of birds on the shaft, including a *garuda*-bird, before releasing it. It was that *garuda* that had obscured the sun when the arrow came down.)

All the people shouted, 'What no one could do, Snotty Joro has been able to achieve. Now let us part and go home!'

But Rogmo Goa cried, 'Wait!' And, with one hand holding the rib joints of 70 sheep, with the other a jar of spirits, together with a turquoise gem the size of a vulture's head, she said, 'I shall have as husband the man who, while I turn my back to the crowd, can distribute to each and all of them the ribs of 70 sheep and the jar of spirits, and, at the same time, put into his mouth this turquoise gem the size of a vulture's head'. She then offered the three things to this one and that one, but no one was able to do anything with them. Only the son of Badmari, Bam Soyurja — a master sorcerer — would have been capable of it, had not Joro, in the meantime, been hiding nearby, robbing him of some of his magic powers so that he, too, was unable to do anything.

When Rogmo Goa approached Joro and saw his nose full of mucus, she turned away and moved on, but uncle Chargin reprimanded her, saying, 'Even though you are fine-looking, you are still a woman. My Joro may be bad-looking, but he is still a strong man. Isn't that so? Has this beauty of yours made you forget that he has defeated your three excellent archers and disposed of your three strong wrestlers?' She then took her three things to Joro who, as soon as he met her, seized them from her hands and said, 'What kind of a fine maiden are you? You would not even notice it if the back of your skirt caught fire! You are but a common and ordinary girl!'

Rogmo turned her back to him. When Joro, with his magic powers, had finished distributing the ribs of the 70 sheep and the jar of spirits to the large crowd of people, and had successfully placed the turquoise gem into his mouth, he sat down. All the people burst out laughing.

Chotong Noyan said, 'However worthless you may be, you, my Joro, son of our beloved brother, have won!' However, from then on, he thought of ways and means to take her away from him.

Section XIV

By now, the people had all but dispersed. Rogmo Goa had collected her followers and fled homewards. She asked her entourage whether the 'ugly man' was getting closer, but they said that no one was in sight. And so they proceeded.

Further on, she asked again whether anyone could be seen in the distance, but they kept on saying, 'Nothing at all'. But Joro, thanks to his magic, had actually reached them and had placed himself on Rogmo's horse, riding pillion. When they saw him, they called out, 'Ah! We see him, he is just sitting behind you!' 'Alas! What shall I do?' she cried, 'I am doomed and in deep trouble. Until now, I have been busy choosing a husband to the point where I have lost all interest. Now what shall I tell my dear parents? How can I face them?' Thus she went on, still lamenting.

Joro then used his magic powers to raise a cloud of dust like that raised by myriad horsemen. Seeing that, Rogmo's parents said, 'Such a huge cloud of dust! It must be Birayan Khan coming with Rogmo as his wife.' Thereupon the dust looked like that stirred up by 1,000 horsemen. 'Perhaps she has married Mirayan Khan', the parents said. When it looked as if the dust was being raised by 900 men they said, 'Is it Chigachin Khan who has taken her?' But when the dust appeared as if it had been stirred by a mere 100 horsemen, the parents said, 'Her husband is probably Chotong Noyan'.

Next, Joro came in a cloud raised by 70 horsemen, to which they said, 'Would that not be Badmari's son Bam Soyurja?' Soon after, as they were still watching, Rogmo Goa arrived with Snotty Joro sitting behind her.[85] The father was furious with his daughter, grabbed his bridle and whip, and went off to his herd of horses through the gate on the right. Rogmo's elder brother, also angry with her, took his bow and arrows and went out to his flock of sheep by the door on the left. The mother, equally enraged, kept looking about while shifting things around. The servants kept moving the cauldron hither and thither. They spread out the saddle cloth, using it as a rug for Joro, but did so incorrectly, so that he had to

85 The names of the new personages mentioned in this section are spelt differently in the various versions of the story and, being fictitious, cannot be identified with real characters.

sit facing the wrong side of the yurt. When they asked him why he was sitting incorrectly on the rug they had laid down for him, Joro replied, 'When riding, which way do you usually place the saddle on the horse?' Whereupon the servants made Joro stand up and spread the rug the right way.

However, Joro quickly moved off and went to sit at Rogmo's table. He said to her, 'Your father went out through the door on the right with bridle and whip. Is it because his herd of horses has been attacked by robbers? I am quite brave. Give me a horse and I shall pursue them and bring him back the haul. Your elder brother went off by the left door with his bow and arrows. Have the wolves perchance attacked his flock of sheep? I am a good marksman. Give me a bow and arrow. I will kill the wolves and bring back their carcasses. Your mother has been looking about, shifting things all over the place. Are your belongings bewitched? I am an expert at countering goblins with cursing-magic. I shall exorcise her utensils. Your servants are moving the cauldron hither and thither. Is the cauldron affected by anthrax? I know a magic spell against it. I will use it and mend the cauldron for them.' So he said, but in the evening Rogmo's parents and the household all got together and started railing at her. 'You wicked and ill-omened girl, bringing us this man of all men! What if one day our dogs will take and devour this wonderful husband of yours? What a misfortune you will have caused to us should this happen!' With these words — full of sarcasm of course — they turned the cauldron upside down, stuck Joro under it and abandoned him there.

During the night, Joro forced himself out of the cauldron, killed a sheep, ate some of the meat, and gave the rest to the dogs. Then he smeared his calf jacket with the sheep's blood and left without it. He went out and spent the night in the open. When Rogmo's parents got up next morning and saw the bloodstained jacket, they said to their daughter, 'Your good husband has been attacked and devoured by the dogs. You alone are responsible for this trouble!' Rogmo sat there filled with inner remorse.

As she was sitting thus, she said to herself, 'The things Joro does are much better and far beyond those that his own body could ever achieve. I wonder whether he is really dead?'

Rogmo Goa went out to look for him. While she was searching, Joro appeared to her magically disguised as a horse-herd tending his herd. She asked him, 'Herdsman, have you seen Snotty Joro?'

The man replied, 'I do not know the one you call "Snotty Joro", but I have heard people say that the three tribes of Tusa, Dungsar, and Lig are now approaching with the aim of inflicting a horrible death on Senggeslü Khan's daughter Rogmo Goa and badly pillaging her parents because she abducted Joro and had him devoured by dogs!' Believing the man's words, Rogmo went on her way in tears.

Then, Joro appeared again to her, transformed into a shepherd guarding his flock of sheep. Having asked him the same question, the shepherd gave her exactly the same reply as before. 'The words of these two men tally: for me there is no other course but to die. However, rather than going back to my parents' home and showing them my miserable end, I shall die alone. I shall end my life by drowning in this river!' So saying, she drove her horse towards a big rock to jump from, but, as she was riding at full speed, Joro, with his magic powers, caught the horse by the tail and held it back. Rogmo turned around and saw him.

'Ah, Joro!' she called, 'Come, mount the horse!' Joro sat on the back, the golden-yellow mucus pouring from his nose.

Rogmo Goa bent forward in revulsion at the snot, crying, 'What are you doing, Joro? Sit back to front!'

Joro then dismounted and said, 'Doesn't a high mountain have its path? Does a living body have a single head, or does it have two? Isn't this the correct way of mounting a horse?' Whereupon he tried to climb over her horse directly from the front.

'No, this is not it.' Joro said, 'Then perhaps this is the right way', he added trying to climb up the horse's hindquarters, but the animal bucked and threw him to the ground.

Rogmo Goa got off the horse and shouted, 'Joro dear, stand up!' Joro kept lying on the ground without uttering a sound. Rogmo begged him again to get up, and Joro at last complied, saying, 'It is up to you whether I sit facing forward or facing backwards!' Rogmo then let him sit behind her facing forward.

After Joro's return, Rogmo Goa's uncle and aunt on her mother's side came to visit her, saying, 'Our niece is the incarnation of a *dakini*-fairy. Let us see whether she has found a good or bad husband.'

Joro's in-laws promptly hid him in an empty storeroom and gave him a bowl full of fried wheat to eat, saying, 'Dear one, do not come out until those people have left'.

As soon as the uncle and aunt arrived they enquired as to what 'our' son-in-law was like. 'How are we to know?' Rogmo's parents replied. 'He is still such a young lad. Today he went to some neighbours who are having a feast.' As they were conversing thus, Joro came out of hiding with yellow slime running from his nose, a grain of wheat hanging at the end of it, and asking what they were saying about him.

Rogmo Goa's uncle and aunt said, 'Damn you all! You bad lot, how can you act like this?'[86] And they returned home, driving the herd of horses along with them.

'Give me a horse, armour, a quiver and a bow! I am quite brave. I shall pursue them and try to catch them!'

So Joro cried, but Rogmo's parents refused, saying, 'How can you expect us to give a horse or anything else to such a good-for-nothing like you?' Thereupon Joro went to the flock of sheep lying around the house, seized a ram and a billy goat, tied them together and with them went in pursuit. He caught up with them, struck both horses and men, took the herd of horses and returned with it.

After all this, Joro said, 'I wish to return to my home!'

'What have you done, you wretch, that we should allow you to return to your home?' railed Rogmo at him. 'Stay here and do nothing of the sort!' Geser then transformed himself into Chotong Noyan while, as Joro, he went off to catch field rats.

In the form of Chotong Noyan, he went to Rogmo's place, dismounted and asked her, 'Where is Joro?'

'Who knows? He went off to catch field rats, didn't he?' she replied.

'I am a great prince, ruler of Tibet', said he. 'You, my good and beloved daughter-in-law, are unhappy. If you want that worthless Joro to be disposed of, I shall kill him. If you want him to be given to another wife, I shall do so. If you want to drive him away, I shall banish him and take you as my wife!'

86 These words can be interpreted differently and as more offensive.

'How can I decide? It is up to you! These are family matters that must be settled among yourselves', Rogmo said.

'I shall take you as my wife because I love you with all my heart!' So saying, Chotong rode off just as Joro came home. 'Who is the one who just rode off?' asked Joro.

'I don't know. He said he was your relative Chotong, that's all', said Rogmo.

'What did he come for?'

'Who knows? He asked for you, mounted his horse and off he went.'

'Our country Tibet is far away from this area', said Joro. 'And why, if he asked for me, did he go off without meeting me?'

'I do not know', replied Rogmo. 'He asked for you and then went on his way.'

'But I know', said Joro twice.

'What do you know, you scoundrel? You say that only to hurt me, isn't that so?' she screamed at him.

'I see that from now on you are going to scare me', said Joro, going out.

The following day, Joro once again transformed himself and came to Rogmo in the shape of Badmari's son, Bam Soyurja, while Joro himself — in his own shape — again went out hunting. As Bam Soyurja he spoke deceptively just like Chotong, declaring his passion for her and, riding off as Joro, returned home.

'Who was that?' asked Joro.

'He said he was Badmari's son Bam Soyurja.'

'What did he want?'

'He asked for you and then rode off.'

'Then why did he not stop and greet me?' said Joro. 'I know why. Some Tibetan bravos got together and decided to kill me. They won't go away until you have given your consent!'

The following day, Geser transformed himself and came in the guise of 30 Tibetan warriors. The weapons they wore were, indeed, most impressive. They dismounted outside Iskilü (= Senggeslü) Khan's dwelling. Someone there asked who those splendid men were.

'We are Tibetans', they replied. 'If you are going to hand us Joro's wife, say so. If you are not going to give her, then say no. We have been sent here to find out from you.'

Iskilü Khan and all his family met to discuss the matter. 'If we say yes', they said, 'how can we live, thinking that we have given away our beloved child to them? If we say no, the 30 warriors will kill us. We must find a way to appease them.'

Accordingly, they replied, 'You go home. We shall send you our daughter as soon as all the preparations are completed.'

To which they said, 'If you regard Joro as a bad proposition and intend to give her in marriage to another man, then give her to us. But if you still refuse to give her away and hold on to Joro, know that these 30 reincarnated heroes can handle others by far superior to you! You foolish people don't give yourselves airs. If you hesitate and delay it is your decision — beware, however, of the consequences!' With these words, they withdrew.

'These words leave us in deadly fear', said Senggeslü, and, as a result, he decided to move camp. Having reached Tibet, he settled down there together with the entire family.

Section XV

Driven again by hate and jealousy, Chotong Noyan made the following announcement: 'Thirty thousand men will gather for a great race. The prize offered consists of a duly consecrated armour,[87] the helmet called Prestigious, the sword called Great Splendour, and the shield called Ten Thousand Stars. All these beautiful objects will be presented at the race and given as prizes to the winning rider. That man will also take Rogmo Goa as his wife!'

87 Lit. '(ritually) sprinkled' (*chabdatu*). Other interpretations are possible. For these weapon prizes cf. see also Section IX, n. 59.

As the 30,000 men were assembling for the race, Joro, making an incense offering, beseeched his heavenly grandmother, Absa Kürje: 'Grandmother of mine! It was in order to help all the creatures in this world that I was born as Geser Khan, Lord of the Ten Quarters. It was in order to deliver from suffering the souls of all the sinners doomed in the hereafter to the realm of Erlig Khan[88] that I was born as Khangkhui Köbegün.[89] Chotong Noyan has assembled 30,000 men for a race so as to steal my own wife. Should my bay foal[90] be of good use to me send it down. If not, send down another horse from the heavenly herd.'

'This is indeed my dear Snotty!' said the grandmother, and sent him down the bay foal transformed into a seven-year-old bay horse. However, because it had come down from the heavens, it kept turning around like a whirlwind and would not let itself be caught by Joro. Not being able to catch it, Joro placed some impure incense on top of the burning incense offering. Because of this impurity in the offering, the bay horse became a mangy, two-year-old bay colt, which could be caught. Riding his mangy colt, Joro followed the 30,000 men, and, on the way, met Senggeslü Khan.

'Ah, my poor son-in-law!' exclaimed Senggeslü, 'Who are you going to overtake with that mangy colt, you midget? Or do you wish that my darling child be taken from you by someone else? Go and join the race riding a gelding from my vast herd!'

'What if the gelding from your vast herd is unwilling to follow my lead?' replied Joro. 'I shall race on my mangy bay colt to which I am accustomed.' He went on and, with the other 30,000 men, arrived at the meeting place at the appointed time.

Together with their horses, they all lined up in readiness and the great race began. Joro restrained the mangy colt with his reins and kept on doing so, eventually loosening them and sending the horse ahead, overtaking the first 10,000 riders. Once again, he restrained his colt, then gave it the reins and overtook another 10,000 riders. He did the same with the third lot of 10,000 men. At a distance of a seed's throw

88 That is, to Hell. See n. 74. Mongolian Erlig = Turkic Erklig 'Mighty'.
89 Another epithet or designation of Joro/Geser, the meaning of which is not clear; possibly 'Prince Joyous' — in contrast to Erlig Khan/Yama, who, as the sovereign ruler of the underworld, was the 'Prince of Sorrow'.
90 See Section IV.

ahead of him, Chotong Noyan was racing on his light bay horse as fast as a gazelle.[91] Ahead of Chotong, on his fine grey horse and at a distance of a whistling arrow's[92] shot, Asmai Noyan raced, by leaps and bounds.

Addressing his mangy bay colt, Joro said, 'I shall charge him, Asmai, under the sign of resolution; you will charge Chotong under the sign of courage. You will strike both horse and rider, trampling on the forelegs of his swift, light bay and so we shall overtake him.'

The colt replied, 'I obey!'

Joro first attacked Chotong, and things happened just as he had said. After being overtaken, Chotong Noyan looked at Joro and cried: 'Alas, Joro, what are you doing?'

'And what are *you* doing, uncle?' replied Joro, adding, 'Someone wants to take my Rogmo!' Joro kept going, while he spoke to his colt: 'My mangy bay colt, which has overtaken 30,000 men, we still have to overtake the grey horse of Asmai Noyan!' So saying, he restrained the colt, then loosened the reins letting him run free. Then, Asmai Noyan's grey courser stretched its head forward and took off, pulling the reins and gnawing at the bridle-bit. Keeping at a distance of a shot of a whistling arrow, it could not be overtaken by Joro, who, in tears, said to his mangy colt, 'Alas, my mangy bay colt, what are you doing? Are you willing to allow that my consecrated armour, the helmet called Prestigious,[93] the sharp sword called Tomarchag, and the shield called Ten Thousand Stars — all these precious adornments to my person — as well as my Rogmo Goa, who, for the past six years has been my close companion, be snatched by someone else?'

'My dear Snotty,' replied the colt, 'I am a heavenly foal and even though that is an earthly horse, it can outdo me four times. It has a lot more hair than me and so I am unable to catch up with it. Take your plea to your heavenly grandmother Absa Kürje!'

91 Lit. '(like) a gazelle overtaking a gazelle'.

92 *Godoli*: a particular type of arrow with a perforated horn-tip which 'whistled' while it flew.

93 See n. 59.

'Grandmother of mine!' cried Joro. 'Your seven-year-old bay horse is below par, and the inferior grey horse of Asmai Noyan is climbing to heaven — he is about to win! Woe is me! Asmai Noyan wishes to seize my many precious adornments and my Rogmo Goa, whom I have won by magical means. Ah! Grandmother of mine, what will you do about it?'

The grandmother heard him and replied, 'Alas, my Snotty Joro is crying because he is going to be overcome by a human being! Boa Dongjong, come here! Try to blow air at the mangy bay colt. I shall try another stratagem with the horse of Asmai Noyan.' Both of them then came down together through the sky. Boa Dongjong blew air at the bay colt, which regained the shape of a seven-year-old bay horse and, stretching the head forward, pulled the reins, gnawing at the bridle-bit. Grandmother Absa Kürje shot a fiery arrow across both the forelegs of Asmai Noyan's grey horse, which tumbled a few times before collapsing.

Joro's former colt continued the race, and, as it approached the goal, Asmai Noyan arose, weeping, and cried, 'Alas! What happened?'

'At first', replied Joro, 'the grey horse got the better of my bay horse, but now luck is on my side!' So saying he reached the goal. He then took those precious ornaments — the victory prizes — gave them to his elder brother, Jasa Shikir, and returned home.

The following day, Chotong Noyan, overcome once more by envy and jealousy, announced that whoever could slay the wild bull[94] and cut off the tail with its 13 vertebrae may win Rogmo Goa. All the people went out. Joro also arrived and shot at the wild bull with a small arrow without a metal tip, and a bow of fir not mounted with horn,[95] hitting him right between the eyes. He then cut off its tail with 13 vertebrae and took it with him.

Chotong Noyan came along and said to Joro, 'My dear Joro, in future I shall never rebuke you and I shall never hit you again. I shall cherish you more than my own offspring. However, let me have the tail of the wild bull with the 13 vertebrae!'

94 Here, the bull (*bukha*) of the text possibly designates the wild ox (*bukha görögesü*), *viz.* the grand extinct auroch (*Bos primigenius*) of Europe, Asia, and North Africa, in particular the Turano-Mongolian subgroup (*Bos primigenius* forma *taurus*).

95 Like the ones used by children when learning archery. This was Joro's ploy for what follows.

'What am I to do with the tail, uncle?' replied Joro, 'I shall give it to you. But, since I have only recently begun to wear a quiver — to learn archery, that is — give me instead one of your *ismanta*-arrows.'[96]

'What am I to do with an arrow?' said Chotong. 'Here, take it!' He gave the arrow to Joro, who, in return, gave him the tail after he had removed three vertebrae from it by magical means.

Chotong Noyan proceeded to the big hunting ground and assembled the hunters. Then in a loud voice he proclaimed, 'I have killed the bull and cut off the tail with its 13 vertebrae. I shall, therefore, take Rogmo Goa as my wife!' In the meantime, Joro had also arrived.

'Alas, alas, uncle Chotong, what a shameful and reprehensible liar you are!' he shouted. 'I have killed the bull, and as I was cutting off the tail with the 13 vertebrae, you came along. Did you not say, "Dear Joro, in future I shall not abuse you nor shall I hit you, but I shall love you more than my own offspring; only let me have this tail?" And did I not say, "What would I do with the tail, uncle? Since I have only recently begun to wear a quiver, give me instead one of your *ismanta*-arrows?" Did you not give it to me saying, "What am I to do with an arrow?"' Thereupon Joro pulled out the arrow and showed it around.

'Look at this infamous character!' exclaimed Chotong. 'When he saw that his wife was going to become mine he stole the arrow from the custodian of my quiver and now he is making all this fuss without reason!'

To which Joro replied, 'If that is so, check now whether you have the entire tail of the bull!' They checked the tail and found that three vertebrae were missing. 'Where are they?' asked Joro. Chotong Noyan kept silent. 'Knowing what a shameful liar you were, I indeed removed the three vertebrae before giving the tail to you!' said Joro, and, at the same time, pulled out from somewhere the three vertebrae in question and also showed them around. Covered with shame, Chotong Noyan turned back and left.

That very night, Joro stole Chotong's precious black horse, which was with his herd of 108 *khainag* cows, and killed it.

---

96 According to some commentators, this was a 'renowned' type of arrow; others claim that it designated a lightweight arrow. However, the name varies in the manuscripts and a contemporary (17th–18th c.) version has *samanda*. I think it transcribes a foreign, probably Persian or Arabic, term. Cf. Persian *samand* 'an arrow'.

The following morning, Chotong Noyan came and made a search in the course of which the flesh of his black horse was found. 'Alas, what happened?' he cried, and forthwith assembled a force of Tibetans and Tanguts in order to kill Joro, but Joro had transformed himself into a big lad with a ruddy face. From his shoulder-strap, he pulled out his Prestigious bow,[97] and as he drew it, it produced a sound like that of a 1,000 roaring dragons, at which Chotong Noyan fled at the head of his men.

Section XVI

The next day, Chotong Noyan again addressed his tribesmen saying, 'Whoever can slay 10,000 bulls during a day's hunt and can then stuff the flesh of these bulls into the stomach of a single bull, and who besides that is capable of crossing the Ugtun River,[98] he is to have Rogmo Goa as wife.' Hence many hunters reassembled.

Since Joro had neither bow nor arrows, Rogmo Goa fetched both from a camel herder and gave them to him, saying, 'Here, take them and see if you can break them!' Joro stretched the bow, which he broke and discarded. Rogmo Goa then took the archery equipment of a cowherd and gave it to Joro, who again broke the bow as he drew it and then discarded it.

Rogmo Goa once more brought him the bow and arrows of a horseherd, and, as he gave them to him, said, 'Dear Joro, if after these you still need bows and arrows, then they would have to be my own ribs!'

When Joro had also broken them and thrown them away he departed and went to the place where the hunters where already shooting at the wild bulls. Joining the hunt, in the course of a day's battue, Joro, thanks to his magic powers, slayed 10,000 bulls and stuffed the stomach of one bull with their chopped flesh. He took the tail of one bull and hung it on a pole, so that, by means of this signal, all the many hunters who had wandered off would rally and follow him.

97 Here, Joro's bow not his helmet is called 'Prestigious' (*daguriskhui*).
98 Thus our text. Other versions call the river Ugtus and Udus (or Odos).

When they reached the river Ugtun, none of the throng could make the crossing. Then Joro came along and took a bull with him, which he drove across the stream. Only the tips of its horns were visible above the water. Then he took a wild ass and drove it across the river — in another spot however — where the water came up to its flanks. He did the same with a gazelle, but by magical means he made the animal look, in Chotong's eyes, like a one-year-old wild boar. Whereupon he declared, 'Now, you three great princes! The three points of crossing have been revealed: choose the one you like!'

'I shall cross the river by the route of the gazelle!' said Chotong Noyan.

'I shall cross it by the route of the wild ass!' said Sanglun.

'And you, uncle Chargin, why are you so silent?' asked Joro.

'My dear Joro,' said Chargin, 'you decide for me!'

'Then you, my uncle Chargin, will cross by the route of the wild ass!' said Joro.

While Sanglun, Chargin, and all the hunters crossed the river by the route of the wild ass, Chotong Noyan decided to follow the route of the gazelle, but he was dragged off by the current. 'Pull me out, dear Joro!' he shouted. Joro seized his whip and rushed into the river. He caught Chotong Noyan by the neck using the whip as a lasso and brought him ashore. 'As for pulling me out you may have done so, dear Joro,' cried Chotong, 'but I have now gained the title of gallows-bird! What can I do about that?'

'Well,' said Joro, 'I had no other choice', and left him there.

Chotong Noyan was struggling again for his life while drifting in the water and kept on shouting. 'Dear Joro, pull me out!' Joro rushed in and, as he was dragging him by the hair, by the time they approached land he had made Chotong quite hairless. On reaching the shore Chotong Noyan once more addressed Joro, saying, 'Dear Joro, you have pulled me out, sure enough, but for that I will receive the title of baldpate! There is nothing I can do about it, is there?'

'Fine!' said Joro, and went off, abandoning him on the spot, whereupon Chotong was again carried away by the current, pleading for dear Joro to pull him out as he was going to die. Joro, however, turned a deaf ear.

Then the people around shouted, 'Poor man, he is going to perish. Dear Joro, do pull him out!'

Joro transformed his whip into a two-edged sword and flung it towards Chotong, who grasped it — with his bare hands. After he had thus been hauled to shore, the palms of both his hands were badly cut.

'Dear Joro,' said Chotong, 'you have pulled me out, but even so, what about the palms of my hands?'

'Right!' replied Joro, 'Although you keep reprimanding and finding fault with me, it's only talk and of no consequence, uncle. Just keep quiet!'

On the road, the hunters had to spend the night in the open. It was very cold, and they had neither wood nor *argal* to burn. Chotong had a dog that understood human speech. He told the dog, 'Go and stay near Joro, and listen to what he says'. Joro, knowing by his magic powers of the dog's coming, said to the hunters, 'Tomorrow we shall set up camp in the Valley of Bows and Arrows. There we can find and lay hands on both. Therefore, you can break your old bows and arrows! When we pitch camp in the Valley of Boots we shall get new boots, so you can hang your boots — the ones you are wearing now — on the horns of your *khainags*! And since any three men can make a tripod to support a cauldron with their knees, you can cook your food and spend the night eating rather than have an empty stomach!'

The dog went back to Chotong Noyan and related precisely all the things Joro had said, whereupon Chotong announced to all his tribesmen: 'Tomorrow, when we enter the Valley of Bows and Arrows we shall get bows and arrows. When we pitch camp in the Valley of Boots we shall get boots. Let three men make a tripod with their knees to support a cauldron so that you can eat prepared food! Do not spend the night with an empty stomach but, as I say, spend it eating proper meals! Get up! I, Chotong Noyan, enjoin you to break your bows and arrows, to make human tripods with your knees to support a cauldron and cook your meals, to hang your boots on the horns of your *khainags* and not spend this night on an empty stomach!'

Accordingly, they all broke their bows and arrows, formed tripods in threesomes with their knees to support the cauldrons and hung their boots on the horns of the *khainags*. However, when the campfires rose and burned their knees, they shouted with pain, tipping up the cauldrons. Thus without any food to cook, they had to spend the night on an empty stomach.

The following day at dawn, Chotong Noyan mounted his horse and went to see Joro. 'Are you there, dear Joro?' he called.

'What is it, uncle?' said Joro, making his appearance.

'Where is your so-called Valley of Bows and Arrows, Joro? Where is the so-called Valley of Boots?' asked Chotong.

'What is the matter, uncle? What kind of talk is this?' said Joro.

'You said that when we camp in the Valley of Bows and Arrows we would find bows and arrows, and that we would find boots when we pitch camp in the Valley of Boots.'

'Who, uncle, told you that?'

'My dog told me,' said Chotong.

'You are certainly an amazing man if you can converse with a dog!' said Joro.

Chotong, full of shame, turned his back and left, but soon after turned round, came back and asked Joro:

'Is it true, dear one, what I heard about you having a dream last night?'

'It is indeed true, uncle!' replied Joro. 'I dreamt that if a black bull is shot down with an arrow this would bring misfortune on us, but it wouldn't matter if it is a bull with a white patch on the forehead.'

At dawn the following morning, the whole tribe organised a big battue. This time, Chotong Noyan complied and did not shoot at black bulls but went in search of a black bull with a white patch on the forehead. Earlier in the morning, a big bull with some hoar frost in the middle of its forehead had rushed past him. Chotong Noyan had chased it, thinking it was a black bull with a white patch. While in pursuit of it, the hoar frost had disappeared from the middle of its forehead. 'This one is black and I have been chasing it by mistake,' said Chotong, and turned back.

After he had rejoined the hunt, a bull with a clump of snow stuck between its horns came running in his direction. 'This is the black one with a white patch!' exclaimed Chotong and chased it.

During the chase, on horseback and with the help of his dog, Chotong managed to corner the bull and drive it close to where Joro was. 'Dear Joro! Darling Joro!' called out Chotong, 'Shoot and kill this bull for me!'

'Alas, uncle of mine, don't you know that I am a bad shot? If I want to shoot at the bull I may hit and kill your horse or your dog. I'd rather not do that!'

'Dear Joro, never mind the horse and the dog: just get the bull, kill it! said Chotong.

'All right, uncle. If that is so, turn the bull around and bring it within my range since my horse is unable to catch up with it', replied Joro.

Chotong Noyan then ensnared the bull and drove it around towards Joro, who, advancing from behind, his bow drawn and, with his magic, shot an arrow that went all the way through Chotong's horse and dog, killing the bull outright.

Chotong Noyan got off the fallen horse and cried, 'Dear Joro, you may have killed the bull, but where are my poor horse and dog?'

'True,' said Joro, 'but what can I say, uncle, only that I am at fault. However, when you spoke to me, didn't I tell you that I was a bad shot!' Joro continued, 'And your bull is not a bull with a white patch on the forehead, it is just a black bull!'

Chotong Noyan checked and exclaimed, 'Oh, dear! What have I done? I thought I hunted a bull with a white patch but instead it was just a black bull. What am I to do, dear Joro?'

'The misfortune caused by this event shall rest with the horse and the dog. You, uncle, be quiet!' said Joro.

'Dear one,' said Chotong, 'That's very good of you!'

It was because Chotong's fine horse and his dog knew human speech that Joro killed them both by magical means.[99]

99 This closing paragraph sounds like an ad hoc justification for the otherwise irrational and gratuitous (in the present context) killing of both the horse and dog of Chotong Noyan.

Section XVII

All the hunters returned to their homes and Rogmo Goa came out to meet them. She asked Chargin who had killed the 10,000 bulls in the one-day hunt, and who had made the crossing of the river Ugtun. Uncle Chargin said, 'Who else could have done it but my Shilu Dasba?'[100]

Rogmo Goa could not understand, and kept asking herself, 'Who is this Shilu Dasba?'

As she did not know that Joro had acquired a title, she again asked, this time posing the same question to uncle Chotong who replied, 'Anyone could have done it. In fact, my eldest boy Altan could have done it!'

'How strange this case is!' said Rogmo Goa and walked away amazed and dismayed.

When Rogmo Goa returned home, Joro came along, riding an ox and carrying a pole, at the end of which a bull's stomach,[101] bespattered with dung, was attached. His mother-in-law went out to meet him. When she arrived, wishing to unload the flesh of the bulls killed by Joro, she had a look, then she turned back shouting, 'Oh woe is me! The hunters have all been lying to me!' She was furious with Joro and before entering her home she threw the bull's stomach with the flesh in it on the roof-ring of the yurt. Suddenly the joints of the roof-ring cracked and the whole yurt collapsed. 'Oh dear!' she cried, 'What is that, son-in-law?'

'It's a filthy stomach', replied Joro, running into the house and extracting with a beam the flesh from the bull's stomach. Meanwhile, the mother-in-law dug out a fireplace and set a cauldron on it. 'My dear,' said Joro, 'the flesh of the bulls I killed won't fit into your single cauldron. You must collect all the caldrons of the neighbourhood to cook it!'

The mother-in-law sent people in all directions to gather the neighbours' cauldrons, had many fireplaces built, provided water for the cauldrons and filled these to the brim with the meat. When the meat was cooked and taken out lots of people assembled for the meal.

---

100 This is another title or epithet given to Geser when he was still the young Snotty Joro. Some commentators render it (from Tibetan) as 'Able and Brave' or 'A Patient Boor (*or* Simpleton)'.

101 Lit. 'the second stomach of a ruminant' (*sarkinag*). The stomach in question was, of course, the one that Joro had stuffed with the flesh of the slain bulls (by magic, as usual) earlier in the story.

Joro's mother-in-law had eaten the meat, which was in one of the sides of the bull's stomach. Joro, with his magical skill, transformed it into a whole bull inside her belly. Unable to digest all that meat insider her, she lay prostrate and close to death. Then, Joro, using a white stick one fathom long, stroked her belly thrice upwards and thrice downwards uttering the words, 'Mother dear, do not die through indigestion!' Soon the mother-in-law relieved herself from both ends and got well again.

Chotong Noyan, who was still filled with hatred and jealousy, issued the proclamation: 'To any man who slays the *garuda*-bird and obtains its two beautiful tail feathers shall be given Rogmo Goa as wife'. A multitude of people travelled from their camps to admire this unusual hunt.[102] Joro's supernatural body[103] had risen to the sky while his lower earthly body was moving about in the world. When he arrived, a large crowd had already assembled. They were shooting arrows at the *garuda* but were unable to hit it. Only Badmari's son, Bam Soyurja,[104] had scored a hit in the very middle of its nest.

Having reached the site, Joro began to flatter the *garuda*. 'How splendid is your roaring voice: your head together with your neck have so much power and beauty', said Joro, causing the bird to display both. 'If the *garuda*'s neck and head are so strong and beautiful,' added Joro, 'how much more so its whole body must be!' Thereupon the *garuda* revealed its entire body. Joro spoke further: 'With your whole body so beautiful, when you fly hither and thither, vigorously flapping your wings, the sight of it cannot be less formidable and charming!'

The *garuda* bird then suddenly took off. Joro drew his bow, shot and brought it down. His supernatural body in the sky picked up the two beautiful tail feathers of the *garuda* and stuck them on Rogmo Goa's headdress. In the meantime, around the *garuda*'s fallen body, all the people were contending with each other in turn over its remaining feathers. Joro was tossed about and pushed away by this or that man, and kept on crying. But it was only a pretence.

102 *Gagcha* (lit. 'alone') *aba*: called like this because the hunter hunted alone with his horse, bow and arrows. To hunt the powerful king of the birds (*garuda*) in this condition must have been regarded as a unique and amazing feat.

103 Joro's 'metamorphic' body (body of transformation) as Khormusda's son.

104 The master sorcerer already mentioned in Sections XIII, XIV, and XVIII.

Rogmo Goa was crying too: 'While the brave men of our people have slain the *garuda*-bird and are giving their womenfolk its feathers to pin on their headdress, my husband Joro is a real pain the way he treats me!'

So Rogmo was lamenting while all the other women were also weeping with her saying,'Poor Snotty Joro has slain the *garuda* and stuck its two beautiful tail feathers on Rogmo Goa's headdress. If only our brave husbands had been so skilful!'

All the people returned to their homes. Only Joro did not return. When Rogmo Goa went back and reached her yurt, as she was about to enter, the two beautiful tail feathers touched the jambs of the doorframe. 'This is odd,' she said to herself, 'how did it happen?' She took off her headdress to have a look and saw the feathers. 'It must have been Joro's supernatural body!' she exclaimed and forthwith she followed his trail.

Geser was sitting in a large rock cave attended by all his guardian spirits. Standing outside and peeping into the cave, Rogmo Goa saw that they were preparing a banquet. She looked and thought, 'Ah, if my husband were as beautiful as Geser!' Whereupon she quickly entered the cave. At that very moment, Geser transformed himself, again assuming Joro's shape.

The White Goddess Ariya Alamkari addressed Rogmo Goa, saying, 'Oh, daughter-in-law, from today on, all the many guardian spirits assembled here will revere you. However, if you are offered any food from this banquet, will you eat it?'

'I will', replied Rogmo Goa.

At the conclusion of the feast, the White Goddess Ariya Alamkari brought a dish with a cooked child in it and offered it to Rogmo Goa, but she refused it. After that, she was offered a dead man's finger. Rogmo Goa cut it, chewed it, and spat it out. Then, the White Goddess asked her, 'What was our agreement?' At that, all the participants of the feast dispersed.

Rogmo Goa, who was at her wits' end, seized Ariya Alamkari by the skirt, who said 'What is that you wish, daughter-in-law?'

'I beg a child from you', said Rogmo.

'Had you eaten that one, you would have borne three sons more outstanding than Geser, three equal to Geser, and three inferior to him, but alas, daughter-in-law, you were unable to do it. Now, how many do you wish to have?'

'You, White Goddess, decide how many you wish to give me!' answered Rogmo Goa.

'You shall have 108', said Ariya Alamkari. She then led Rogmo Goa to her home and withdrew.

Section XVIII

After Joro had gone out, Rogmo Goa wept. Addressing her mother-in-law, she said, 'Oh mother dear, for so long now I have been suffering in all possible ways because your son is not living with me in the accustomed way — as husband and wife do. It would be better for me to die rather than keep on suffering thus. I shall make a complaint about it to Erlig Khan! The white of my eyes has grown yellow, the black of my eyes has turned pale!' With these words she went out.

After Rogmo Goa had left, Joro's mother called him in. He came and she said to him, 'Your wife, Rogmo Goa says that she wishes to die. She says that from time past until now she has suffered endlessly. She wants to report the matter and leave the decision to Erlig Khan. Now, instead of causing the death of someone else's daughter and earning a bad name for myself, you, my dear, should live in the accustomed way with her!'

Joro left and went to lie down in the shape of Geser. Rogmo Goa, who had been watching outside, rushed inside and threw herself upon Geser, whereupon he told her, 'The accustomed way is for a man to lie on the woman, not the other way round!' He then made her turn her face in four directions while he imparted her nine 'instructions'[105] for each directions, 36 in all. They were:

'When I was born a devilish black raven used to peck the eyes of one-year-old children, thus blinding them. Fixing my nine-pronged iron catching-pole on one eye I caught the black raven devil and killed it. Did I not then reveal myself as Geser Khan by adding one eye to my eyes?'[106]

'In my second year, a devil with teeth like those of a goat, a dog's snout, and the shape of an iron beast had transformed himself into the Güngü Echige Ergeslong lama. He used to bite off the tip of the tongue of children, thus making them dumb. When I clenched my 45 snow-white teeth and lay down without suckling, he asked my parents, "Is your child like this from birth or has he become like this only recently?" "At birth", they replied, "he had a mouth and nose. Whether he has just died and become like this we don't know." Thereupon the lama allowed me to suck his tongue. I pretended to suck it a little. "Good, he is sucking it!" said he and gave me much more tongue to suck. Still pretending to suck it, I bit his tongue right at its very root with my 45 snow-white teeth and killed him.[107] Did I not, then, in my second year, reveal myself as Geser Khan by adding a tongue to his tongue?'

'When, in my third year, the accursed field rats changed the face of the earth and did much harm to the Mongolian people, I changed into an old shepherd,[108] took my small steel axe and went off, only to find out that those cursed voles had grown into brown oxen. Then, in the guise of an old cowherd, I struck the oxen between the horns and dispatched them all. When in my third year, I killed the accursed field rats that had changed the face of the earth, causing much harm to the Mongolian people, did I not then reveal myself as the merciful, wise and holy Geser Khan, Lord of the Ten Quarters?'

105 *Surgal üge*. That is, the words of advice and admonition, set mainly in metaphorical form as rhetorical questions, the purpose of which was to affirm beyond doubt that Joro was not a mere human endowed with supernatural powers, but a heavenly being, the divine Geser Khan, entrusted with a superhuman task on earth, *viz.* to become its ruler and eradicate evil. However, the accounts of Geser's former exploits used as illustration and 'teaching' (*surgal*) do not always correspond exactly to those related in the earlier sections, and some are mentioned here for the first time.

106 See Section IV. Geser's additional 'eye' was, metaphorically his catching-pole.

107 See *loc. cit.*

108 See Section IV for the earlier account of this episode, in which Geser had changed into an old cowherd, not into a shepherd, as confirmed a few lines down. 'Shepherd' is a scribal error.

'In my fourth year, I went to the Boljumur Valley. There the Seven Ogres daily devoured 700 men and 700 horses irrespective of their predestined fate. In my incarnation as Joro, I plunged these Seven Ogres into the ocean, killing them. Then there were the 300 Sartagchin common menials and robbers; and the *manggus*-ogre called (Ir) Tonggorog. By killing them all[109] did I not reveal myself as the merciful, wise and holy Geser Khan, Lord of the Ten Quarters?'

'In my fifth year, I went to the Engkerekü Ridge, which, after settling there, I turned into a beautiful and prosperous encampment. As for the 500 merchants of the Erdeni Khan at Olum Tala,[110] with my magic powers I made three days last one day and caused intense heat, while surrounding them with swarms of stinging bees and wasps and depriving them of water. Having thus requisitioned their services, and in order to show gratitude to my parents, I built the temple of the Qomsin bodhisattva. By turning the Engkerekü Ridge into a beautiful and prosperous encampment, did I not reveal myself as the holy Geser Khan?'

'When I was six years old, you, Rogmo Goa, came, bringing along with you three excellent archers and three strong wrestlers.[111] On your arrival and in the presence of a large gathering of men, you declared yourself Rogmo Goa, the incarnation of a *dakini*-fairy. I then killed your three strong wrestlers and defeated in archery your three excellent archers. I confused the minds of 30,000 men and I won you.[112] Driven again by hate and jealousy, Chotong Noyan had announced that 30,000 men would gather for a great race and that the prize consisted of a duly consecrated armour, the helmet called Prestigious, the sword called Great Splendour, and the shield called Ten Thousand Stars. All these beautiful objects would be presented at the race and given as a precious reward to the winning rider. That man would also take Rogmo Goa as his wife. Thus, as all the people assembled I made an incense offering and prayed to my heavenly grandmother Absa Kürje. I rode my spirited

109 In the earlier account, Joro does not kill the 300 Sartagchin. However, he forced them to convert to Buddhism thereby causing them to renege their past behaviour.

110 Cf. Section X, where the account of this event is somewhat different. The 'Erdeni Khan of Taski' in the original account is now the 'Erdeni ("Precious") Khan at Olum Tala ("Olum Plain")', and in the present passage, the merchants are referred to as 'artists (*or* craftsmen)' (*urad*), although three lines further on, they are designated as 'merchants' again. The confusion no doubt arose from the fact that those merchants were subsequently employed by Geser as artists and craftsmen.

111 See Section XIII.

112 This reference is to the event immediately following. See Section XV.

bay horse and overtook the 30,000 men at the contest. I took the many precious ornaments — the fruit of my victory — and gave them to my elder brother Jasa Shikir.[113] As I subdued all in my power, am I not, then Geser Khan the All-Powerful?'

'In my seventh year, Chotong Noyan, overcome once more by envy and jealousy, announced that whoever could shoot and slay the wild bull and be the first in cutting off its tail with 13 vertebrae, that man would win Rogmo Goa.[114] All the people went out. I arrived from the back and shot at the wild bull, hitting it right between the eyes with a small arrow without a metal tip and a bow of fir not mounted with horn. Thereupon I cut off its tail with 13 vertebrae and took it with me. I had all the people subdued by my power and sent Chotong home in shame: am I not, then, Geser Khan the Skilful?'

'In my eighth year, Chotong Noyan again announced that whoever could slay 10,000 bulls during a day's hunt and cross the Ugtun River, he would have Rogmo Goa as wife.[115] Chotong Noyan and all his tribesmen went out. Riding my mangy bay horse, I, as Joro, in the course of a day's battue, shot and killed 10,000 bulls and, furthermore, crossed the river Ugtun. Did I not then reveal myself as the merciful and holy Geser Khan, Lord of the Ten Quarters?'

'In my ninth year, Chotong Noyan, still filled with hatred and jealousy, proclaimed that any man who could shoot and kill the *garuda*-bird and obtain its two beautiful tail feathers, that man shall take Rogmo Goa as wife.[116] All the hunters travelled to admire the spectacle. I, as Joro, was moving about in the world while my supernatural body had risen to the sky. When I arrived, all the people were already shooting arrows at the *garuda* but were unable to hit it. Only Badmari's son, Bam Soyurja, had scored a hit in the very middle of its nest. When, soon after, I came along, I flattered the *garuda*, and while it was vigorously flapping its wings and was about to fly hither and thither, I quickly shot it right through the head, killing it there and then. With my supernatural body, I picked up its two beautiful tail feathers and stuck them on you. Did I not then reveal myself as Geser Khan the Skilful Who Beats All Archers?'

113 See Section XV.
114 See Section XV.
115 See Section XVI.
116 See Section XVII.

'In my 10th year, when I built the temple of the Qomsin bodhisattva to return my parents' favours,[117] was I not the holy Geser Khan? And when, in my 11th year, I seized and killed the devil called Rogmo Nagbo, lord of nasty ailments, was I not Geser the Well-To-Do?'[118]

'When in my 12th year I caught and slew the devil with the iron earring, lord of hydropsy, and in this way put an end to the swelling of dropsy, did I not reveal myself as Geser Khan, Lord-of-All?'

'In my 13th year, when I killed the swell-headed devil, lord of anthrax, thus putting an end to carbuncles, was I not Geser the Holy?'

'In my 14th year I, as Geser,[119] went to a battue with Aju Mergen, the daughter of the king of the dragons. While we were advancing together, I came across seven wild bulls. I shot all seven right through so that they were pinned to the ground. Afterwards, Aju Mergen encountered nine wild bulls and she did the same. Then I kept thinking to myself, "How am I to find out whether Aju Mergen is a man or a woman?" In the meantime, however, I encountered another bull, and, although I was unable to hit it, I managed to chase it away from the midst of the people — from the other hunters, that is. Aju Mergen was hunting behind me. When I looked back and saw her I said, "You are a woman, the person behind me looks just like an ordinary woman!"

'To which she said, "Ah, if you only knew what kind of a woman I am!" and she slew the bull with one shot. I went there, pulled out the arrow, placed it under my armpit and lay down as if I were dead.'

'Aju Mergen said, "Yesterday I killed Temür Khadai, son of Amatai, and seized his grey horse. And today, as it turned out, I killed Geser Khan, Lord of the Ten Quarters, and acquired his brown horse!" With these words, she led the horse away while I lay motionless.'

'Then, with my magic powers, I changed into a different person who shouted, "Because Aju Mergen has killed Geser Khan, Lord of the Ten Quarters, his elder brother Jasa Shikir and the people of the three tribes[120] have assembled and are bent on killing her and causing havoc!"'

---

117 See Section X.

118 The episode in question is not related in the book like the ones that follow it. One gains the impression that these last feats are tall stories told simply to impress and amuse Rogmo Goa.

119 From here on, Geser, in the account of his exploits with Aju Mergen, refers to himself as Geser Khan or, simply, Geser. We have continued to employ in all cases the pronoun 'I'.

120 See Section II.

'Whereupon Aju Mergen untied her hair that she had concealed, saying, "May my right plait not bring bad luck to my father and brother!" and she let the right side of her hair fall down. Then saying, "May my left plait not bring bad luck to my mother and sister!" she let the left side of her hair fall down. Further saying, "May my pigtail not bring bad luck to my Chinese slave!" she let her pigtail fall down her back.'

'When I realised the truth — that she was indeed a woman — I jumped up and wrestled with her. On the first encounter, I fell on my knees. I said, "Surely, in a wrestling match, a man has three chances in succession: does he not stir up the dust four times?" So I wrestled with her once more and threw her down. I said, "I'll take you as my wife!" When she agreed I continued, "If so, will you lick my little finger?" She also agreed. I pricked my little finger and let her lick the blood. Then we went together to the great lake to drink water. As we reached the lake, I saw the reflection of an arrow glisten in the water and said to myself, "There was no one behind me stretching a bow charged with an arrow!" Then I looked behind me and saw Aju Mergen with her tautened bow. "Why are you doing that?" I asked her.'

'She replied, "I am not stretching the bow towards you; I do it to hit a fish in the lake". True to her words, the water of the lake grew red from the dying fish that had just been hit.'

'After we had reached the lake and drunk of its water, I took off my clothes and swam to the other bank. As Aju Mergen could no longer bear to sit and wait for me, she took off her clothes and jumped into the lake. I knew that, so I whistled and a wind rose which turned into a whirlwind that left her clothes hanging from the top of a tree. I then returned and was just putting on my clothes when Aju Mergen came and attacked me, forcing her way under my robe.'[121]

When Geser had imparted these nine instructions for each of the four directions — 36 in all — he said, 'By taking as my wife the daughter of the king of the dragons in my 14th year, did I not reveal myself as the holy and wise Geser Khan of the Ten Quarters? And that in my 15th year I can thunder like a god and roar like a dragon just proves that this is what I am!' So saying he produced the thundering clap of

121 The Mongolian *deel* or long gown worn by both men and women. The long list of Geser's 'didactic' exploits ends on a romantic note.

a god and the roar of a dragon accompanied by a downpour of life-giving ambrosia.[122] While Geser spoke, Rogmo Goa kept on crying and laughing in succession.

This is the first book which spreads the fame and glory of the merciful, holy and wise Geser Khan, Uprooter of Evil in the Ten Quarters.

122 In China, dragons are traditionally associated with rain. And in Shamanism, thunder has always been regarded as the 'voice of Heaven', and later, in Buddhism, as that of the gods, the same Turco-Mongolian word (*tengri*) being used for both 'Heaven' and 'god(s)'.

www.ingramcontent.com/pod-product-compliance
Lightning Source LLC
Chambersburg PA
CBHW041755010726
47507CB00015B/388

* 9 7 8 1 7 6 0 4 6 0 8 2 2 *